KORN/FERRY INTERNATIONAL
powered by LOMINGER

Selecting an

Agile
Leader

Find Future-Ready Talent Today

J. Evelyn Orr and George S. Hallenbeck Jr.

Selecting an Agile Leader

Find Future-Ready Talent Today

ISBN 978-1-933578-48-4

Item number 82206

1st Printing April 2013

Table of Contents

Introduction

There are certain jobs where almost nothing
you can learn about candidates before they start
predicts how they'll do once they're hired.
So how do we know whom to choose in cases like that?

Malcolm Gladwell – British-Canadian journalist and bestselling author

Build or buy? It's the perennial talent question.

The underlying assumption of the build versus buy choice is that talent is an investment without a guaranteed return, no matter which route you take. This is why it's a dilemma.

To build talent requires tremendous investment, patience, and risk tolerance. Investment in development courses and mentors. Patience to allow for experiences and lessons to accumulate and crystallize. Risk tolerance that enables people to take jobs where they'll need to build skills in real time.

To buy talent is also a tremendous investment, especially for leadership roles. Going outside for key roles is time consuming and expensive. Hiring external candidates can be risky. How quickly can the incoming leader get up to speed and accelerate his or her contribution? Will he or she be a good culture fit? Will he or she avoid the minefield of potential derailers that too often trip up executives in transition?

But beyond the build or buy dilemma, there is the question of what to do when the job itself exists in a changing and ambiguous context. When failure is not an option but requirements for success are ill-defined, what do you build? When the job requires a leader to surmount challenges in uncharted territories or when no one has the exact skill set or the precise background or the right experiences, what do you buy?

The build or buy dilemma is not new, but it now exists against a new and unfamiliar backdrop. Global financial uncertainty, regional conflicts, corporate scandals, disruptive technology, and globalization are a few of the multitude of external pressures that organizations are facing in the 21st century. How does a company develop a business strategy and execute to win in such a dynamic and volatile environment?

In order to stay in front of these pressures and uncertainties, many companies are responding by speeding up their own innovation and growth strategies. Often, this approach manifests itself as rapid change and continuous reinvention of brand identity, products, and customer value proposition. Companies know the stakes: change or else. Examples abound of companies who suffered the consequences when they did not adapt and innovate fast enough: Circuit City, Borders, and Kodak, to name a few.

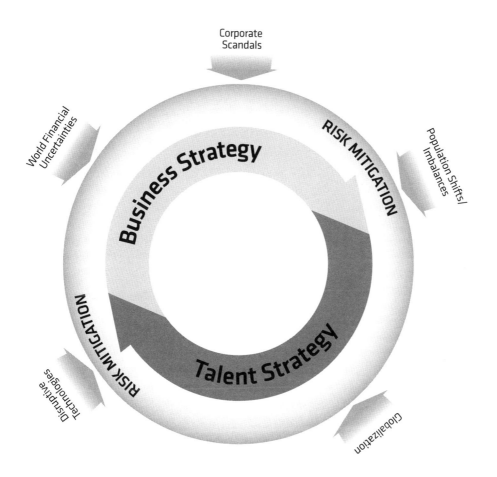

So where does talent come into play? A company's business strategy and talent strategy are interrelated.

Business strategy challenges such as...

underperformance,

lack of organizational capability to
manage innovation and absorb change, and

too much operational focus
detracting from a strategic focus

...can stem from corresponding talent strategy issues such as...

not enough bench strength,

poor hiring and promotion practices, and

ineffective talent deployment and allocation.

The dynamic interplay between business strategy and talent strategy also poses challenges to individual leaders. Jobs are getting bigger (and more complex), successors are getting younger, tenure is getting shorter. The traditional climb up the career ladder is becoming a thing of the past. Mastering the tasks and responsibilities at one level in order to move to the next level is no longer a guarantee of success. Job success today and in the future will depend on talent that can effectively navigate the unfamiliar, the ambiguous, and the complex. Organizations often refer to this type of talent as high-potential talent.

Right about now you may be thinking, "Well, if a candidate has performed well in the past, why can't I assume that high performance will continue?" In fact, past performance is a great predictor of future performance, but only when future challenges mimic past challenges. For better or for worse, that tends not to be the case. This is why the distinction between high performers and high potentials is such a critical part of any talent management strategy. While the majority of high potentials are high performers, only a fraction of high performers are high potentials. The trick is figuring out how to identify the high potentials. What criteria should be used?

Identifying the special quality that high potentials possess can be elusive, especially when we have no prior experience with the person. This is where the concept of Learning Agility enters the scene. Learning Agility is one component that defines potential—but it is a major component. Potential is determined in part by a candidate's "raw material" (i.e., intelligence, emotional intelligence, career ambition) and the sum and quality of his or her experiences (i.e., job changes, key assignments, hardships, relationships with mentors, education). But the factor that makes a dramatic difference in the equation is the candidate's Learning Agility—his or her ability and willingness to learn from experience and apply those lessons to future challenges. When combined with the foundation of the candidate's experiences, abilities, and ambitions, Learning Agility exponentially increases a candidate's potential. This is why Learning Agility is referred to as the Magic Multiplier.

Learning Agility: The Magic Multiplier

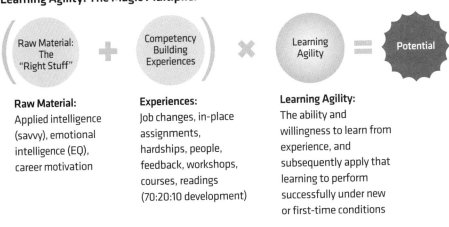

Raw Material:
Applied intelligence (savvy), emotional intelligence (EQ), career motivation

Experiences:
Job changes, in-place assignments, hardships, people, feedback, workshops, courses, readings (70:20:10 development)

Learning Agility:
The ability and willingness to learn from experience, and subsequently apply that learning to perform successfully under new or first-time conditions

Let's return to the dilemma of what talent to build or buy. For many jobs in today's business environment, particularly leadership roles, the short answer to this dilemma is: find internal or external candidates with higher levels of Learning Agility. The purpose of this book is to help you identify talent high in Learning Agility so you are poised to make the best talent decisions.

So how do you know if you're interviewing someone who has the potential to succeed in a new and challenging assignment? At times, detecting Learning Agility can be an exercise in counterintuitiveness. Candidates whom you might label as late bloomers or nomadic wanderers with no clear linear career progression or focus are quite possibly individuals who are following the zigzag career path so commonly found on the resumes of learning agile candidates.

Common Talent Myths

To spot the talent you are looking for, you first need to view individuals through a clear lens. Myths and misperceptions can cloud talent identification and selection efforts. By dispelling the common myths listed below, you will be better prepared to be a more objective assessor of talent.

Smarter people always make better leaders

Intelligence does predict job performance,[1] but leadership is a complex task that involves more than just pure cognitive abilities. IQ also needs to be balanced with EQ.[2] Most executives share a comparable level of intellect, therefore intelligence alone does not discriminate well between good and not-so-good candidates (i.e., derailed executives are as smart as other executives). Recent research suggests that Learning Agility is a better predictor of performance than intelligence, especially in leadership roles.[3]

The most technically qualified person, the one who knows the most about the content of the job, is the best choice for the leadership position

For many decades, individuals with a combination of the most seniority and highest level of technical skill were promoted into leadership roles. In many cases, their skills proved valuable for solving problems, and they could also be mentors to less experienced employees. However, assessing the abilities of technical experts to adapt to new challenges and shifting circumstances, to lead change, and to provide a compelling vision to motivate others is often overlooked. These characteristics are independent of technical skill and also need to be taken into account when evaluating a leader's potential.

Good or bad references indicate the quality of the candidate

References cannot be counted on as reliable sources of information. In some cases, they are hesitant to confirm anything beyond the basic facts about a candidate for fear that they might become the target of a lawsuit if something they say hurts a candidate's chances. Also, personal biases and hidden agendas can positively or negatively influence the referent's comments. Finally, since candidates usually nominate their references, they are likely to be individuals with a strong, positive inclination toward the candidate.

Past performance predicts future performance

There is an often-repeated statement: "The best predictor of future behavior is past behavior." This is a reliable assumption in a limited way: it is true only if the person is being hired for the exact same set of responsibilities performed in his or her previous job. Unless the expectations and the demands of the environment are alike, a different set of skills will be needed for success. Identifying candidates who have exhibited Learning Agility in the past is one way to ensure that the person you hire will have the ability to flex and adapt to changing circumstances and requirements.

The "right" work experience makes a qualified candidate

True, experiences can have a powerful shaping force on development. But the experience itself is not enough. The individual also needs to have acquired some significant lessons from the experience and had the opportunity to apply and refine those lessons in different situations. This is the essence of Learning Agility, which can be assessed through the interview approach outlined in this book.

They came from a top school/company, so they must be good

Mediocre employees can come from world-class companies, and superstars can emerge from bottom-rung competitors. The same reasoning applies to educational credentials and lineage: in the end, it all comes down to the individual and what he or she took away from past experiences, good or bad.

Younger people are more agile and adaptable

Not only is Learning Agility a key way to differentiate talent, it knows no bounds. Research has shown that age, race, global region, culture, and gender have no bearing on whether someone is more or less likely to be learning agile.[4]

What Is Learning Agility?

Learning Agility is the *ability and willingness to learn from experience, and subsequently apply that learning to perform successfully under new or first-time conditions.* It's a willingness to seek out new experiences, a comfort level with ambiguous circumstances, an exploratory mind-set, and a tolerance for making mistakes—knowing those mistakes will add to the ever-expanding catalogue of "lessons I've learned."

Learning agile individuals distinguish themselves during transitions from the known to the unknown—like taking a new job or a promotion, for example. When facing novel, unfamiliar situations, many people revert to their favorite solutions and overapply something that worked in the past. Pioneers in Learning Agility, Bob Eichinger and Mike Lombardo studied patterns of executive success and failure. From their extensive research, they observed that "many of us are more likely to rely on our successful habits from the past rather than going to the trouble of creating new ones. Under the pressure of change or first-time situations for us, we stick to our comfort zone, repeating what has worked before or switching to a different past solution, but not a new strategy."[5]

In novel, unfamiliar situations, when our existing routines and habits may be inadequate, Learning Agility provides the openness and flexibility to learn new ways of coping with unforeseen problems and opportunities. Put another way, high learning agile individuals "know what to do when they don't know what to do."[6]

Learning Agility is not a fixed trait; it is something that can be encouraged, practiced, and learned. Learning agile individuals excel in some combination of five areas—the Learning Agility factors. Throughout the book, we will explore how to observe and assess behaviors consistent with these five factors, in addition to Overall Learning Agility.

Self-Awareness

They know what they're good at
and not so good at and actively
address the not so good

Mental Agility

They are critical thinkers who are comfortable
with complexity, examine problems carefully,
and make fresh connections that they
make understandable to others

People Agility

They understand the value of getting
things done through others and are
exceptional communicators who see conflict
as an opportunity rather than a problem

Change Agility

They like to experiment and can deal
with the discomfort of change; they
have a passion for ideas and are highly
interested in continuous improvement

Results Agility

They deliver results in first-time
situations through resourcefulness
and having a significant presence
that inspires others

When Is It Important to Select for Learning Agility?

Many organizations use Learning Agility as a key part of their talent management strategy. Learning Agility can help your organization shore up its succession slate and populate the talent pipeline because Learning Agility provides a shared definition and common measurement of what it means to be high potential.

Learning Agility can help your organization differentiate its talent. It helps you know whom you're dealing with and how to treat them. High potentials need to be engaged and developed differently from other employees—something that is often described in talent management circles as "differential development." In this way, using Learning Agility as an indicator of potential can help you drive productivity and engagement for your current high potentials and increase your employee value proposition to attract new top talent.

Learning Agility can help you ensure success when you place candidates into "can't afford to fail" roles. This is a matter of risk mitigation. For new or changing roles that will lead to new, high-risk ventures or maybe a desperately needed turnaround, your organization needs learning agile leaders at the helm. Leaders who are able to deal with the ambiguity and complexity so common in uncharted territory.

Learning Agility is a key success differentiator for roles that are new, change-driven, or require fresh ideas and new ways of thinking, including many leadership positions. But it is important to note that not every job requires loads of Learning Agility. Think of roles that require deep expertise and specialization—medical doctors, air traffic controllers, heads of finance, nuclear power plant operators, or engineers. When depth of knowledge and experience is most important, assess for high mastery and deep expertise. When breadth of knowledge and experience is most important, assess for Learning Agility.

Selecting only learning agile candidates is a losing long-term strategy.[7] High learning agile people represent a small portion of the population. So an unsustainable amount of resources would have to be dedicated to finding candidates who fit that profile. But even if a majority of hires were highly learning agile, it's possible to have too much of a good thing. Learning agile talent tends to shake things up, challenge the status quo, and continuously experiment with new approaches. This can create instability and stress for those around them. Consider carefully which roles need more Learning Agility and which roles need less of it.

Given the climate described earlier that so many organizations are facing, many roles do require some modicum of Learning Agility. To evaluate whether a role requires a higher or moderate amount of Learning Agility, consider the following questions:

Does the job involve...

Creativity, fresh ideas, and new ways of thinking?

Operating in a quick-changing field or area of the business where the future is undefined or emerging?

A high level of strategic thinking?

Ongoing collaboration with multiple stakeholders?

Taking charge and implementing new initiatives and change efforts?

Making high-stakes decisions?

Handling difficult people issues?

Confronting others when tasks or projects don't go well?

High visibility and high personal pressure?

Influencing or negotiating with others to win their support?

If you answered a definitive yes to the majority of these questions, Learning Agility is a key factor for success in that role. Someone higher in Learning Agility would likely be the best fit.

If you answered yes to some of these questions, a typical amount of Learning Agility will be useful in that role.

If you answered yes to only a couple of these questions, we recommend that you concentrate on assessing other qualities of the candidate because Learning Agility is less important.

In order to assess Learning Agility, organizations may choose to use a self-assessment, a multi-rater assessment, or a structured interview. This book focuses on assessing Learning Agility through interviews and introduces the structured interview process used in the Learning From Experience™ Interview Guide.

What Factors of Learning Agility Are Most Important?

For long-term career success, all Learning Agility factors are important. For a specific job, all Learning Agility factors are critical to some extent, but the characteristics of the job and what needs to be accomplished may elevate the importance of some factors over others.

Keep reading and you'll learn more about how you can identify and assess the qualities of Learning Agility in the candidates you interview.

When the job involves...

Sensitive interpersonal or intercultural interactions, keen awareness of your limitations, emotional stability and resilience... **Self-Awareness**

Complex, ambiguous problems, creativity and innovation, fresh connections, new ways of looking at persistent problems, seeing both the whole picture and its parts, competing perspectives... **Mental Agility**

Working with new or difficult people, collaborating across boundaries, influencing without authority, diverse cultures and backgrounds, understanding different points of view, customer service... **People Agility**

Conceiving and implementing a vision, making difficult trade-offs, turning around a failing business, starting a new venture, passion and commitment, changes in strategic direction... **Change Agility**

Tight deadlines, high expectations, major obstacles, limited resources, inexperienced or unmotivated teams, key dependencies, unpopular or impossible tasks... **Results Agility**

How to Use This Book

Whether you are a manager, a talent management professional, a recruiter, or an executive, this book is designed to help you better assess a candidate's Learning Agility. The next chapter, "The Science Behind Selection: Why We Can't Completely Trust Our Gut (or Our Mind)," builds the case for a structured interview and assessment methodology. It also outlines some common shortcuts and misperceptions that can bias an interviewer's assessment of Learning Agility.

The heart of the book is centered around the five factors of Learning Agility: Self-Awareness, Mental Agility, People Agility, Change Agility, and Results Agility, beginning with a chapter on Overall Learning Agility. The chapters begin with a definition of the key behaviors and mind-sets associated with that factor. Each chapter features an excerpt from an interview of a well-known person who is an exemplar of that particular agility, building upon the portraits of individuals highlighted in *Becoming an Agile Leader*.

Written with the interviewer in mind, the factor chapters delve into what high, typical, and low Learning Agility looks like. This content provides reference points that can help you draw meaningful conclusions about a candidate's level of agility. The quoted comments, interview examples, and detailed behaviors in each chapter are from actual interviews we have conducted using the Learning From Experience™ Interview Guide.

The last chapter, "Selecting for Learning Agility: How to Use the Learning From Experience™ Interview Guide," explores how to use the Learning Agility interview method. In addition to how to conduct the interview and evaluate the candidate, we discuss when to use the Learning From Experience™ Interview Guide and how it can complement assessment and selection practices already in place in your organization.

One of the best ways to enhance your ability to conduct Learning Agility interviews is to apprentice with an expert. While ideal, that is not always practical or possible. This book is designed to be a resource for interviewers who are new to the Learning From Experience™ Interview Guide, interviewers seeking to sharpen their ability to assess Learning Agility, and interviewers looking for a way to calibrate how they are assessing candidates.

In all, the content of this book was designed to be a springboard—a resource that boosts your confidence and ability to assess individuals' Learning Agility. This is a skill that will help you identify the right talent to successfully lead through the new and unfamiliar challenges that lie ahead.

The learning promise is huge.

It does seem to be the silver bullet of success.

Mike Lombardo and Bob Eichinger
– Founding partners, Lominger International

The Science Behind Selection: Why We Can't Completely Trust Our Gut (or Our Mind)

Many people are overconfident, prone to place too much faith in their intuitions.

Daniel Kahneman – Israeli American psychologist and winner of the 2002 Nobel Memorial Prize in Economic Sciences

Before we take you on a guided tour of the behaviors that differentiate high learning agile people, let's talk about why we need to be careful when we make hiring decisions. If someone asked you what separates humans from other animals in the animal kingdom, you might cite humans' cognitive abilities such as language, reasoning, judgment, and decision making. Indeed, these systems are highly evolved, but as psychologists have discovered over the last several decades, our brains continue to prefer to operate in a default mode. That default mode is "autopilot." Our brains have developed numerous shortcuts that help us expend less energy, pay less attention, and make decisions more efficiently (though not necessarily more effectively).

Much has been written on the concept of mindfulness in an attempt to build our awareness of how we are operating in the world, how we think, and how we come to different conclusions.[8] Taking a mindful approach to interviewing and evaluating people involves building an awareness of the shortcuts, pitfalls, ruts, and biases with which our minds have grown so comfortable.

Cognitive psychologists Daniel Kahneman and Amos Tversky explore how our minds work. Their research has led them to believe that we have a few tools in our toolbox that we go to over and over again when gathering information and drawing conclusions about the world around us. In general, these tools are designed to help us make more efficient and accurate judgments. It is when we overapply them that we get into trouble. In fact, when we are not scrutinizing our thinking, these tools can lead our minds to overlook facts, logic, rational argument, and statistical probability.[9] These are powerful reminders for how the tools we rely on can take over and drive our thinking.

In an essay for the *New Yorker*,[10,11] Malcolm Gladwell pondered, "The job interview has become one of the central conventions of the modern economy. But what, exactly, can you know about a stranger after sitting down and talking with him for an hour?" Gladwell marveled that after a short conversation with a complete stranger, he felt confident that this person was smart and would be successful at most anything. Psychologists Nalini Ambady and Robert Rosenthal confirmed the power of first impressions by showing that these impressions are formed in a flash and not likely to change when observation time is extended.

So what is our initial impression based upon and is it accurate? And, more importantly, when we make initial judgments about someone, are we judging them on the qualities that will matter most for the job we are hiring them to do?

Our minds want to make the leap that "a good impression makes a good candidate." But our radar is picking up a certain set of skills and qualities that are not the whole picture of the person. These qualities we pick up on in the flash of a first impression may not be the qualities that will make this person successful on the job. Does a firm handshake make a good salesperson? That's one possible indicator. Does someone with a warm demeanor make a good teacher? Again, it's possible. But with these flashes of judgment, there are many questions that remain. Does the candidate meet the success criteria for the job?

Structured interviews focus on key success criteria and can help guard against making these leaps of judgment. Research shows that as interview structure increases, the influence of candidates' impression management efforts decreases.[12] In other words, when you know what you're looking for in an interview and you ask the right questions, you are less likely to be influenced by a firm handshake, a nice suit, or a dazzling smile.

One of the reasons it is so important to be mindful of our shortcuts and biases is because, in general, we tend to be overly confident in the accuracy of our decisions and judgments (unjustifiably so). We believe that our assumptions are correct, we see evidence that confirms our beliefs more readily than evidence that refutes our beliefs, and we have trouble even remembering that there were alternative possibilities outside of the one we landed on.[13] For these reasons, it's healthy to question yourself, your rationale, and feel a little more tentative about the conclusions you arrive at.

Beyond first impressions, there are many more decision-making shortcuts we rely on every day. The eight listed here contribute to common judgment errors when we interview candidates. Building awareness of how these shortcuts operate and when we rely on them can limit their biasing influence. That way, critical decisions—such as hiring decisions—can be made in a conscious, unbiased way.

Memorable bookends (a.k.a. the primacy/recency effect). We are more likely to focus attention on the beginning and the end of the interview. Given the way our memories are formed, things that happen early or late in an interaction tend to leave the strongest impression. The observations that are made at the beginning, middle, and end of the interview are equally valid and important. Take care that what happens at the bookends does not grab a disproportionate amount of your attention.

Halos versus horns (a.k.a. the halo effect). When someone leaves a strong impression on us (whether positive or negative), it's common to generalize that impression to all aspects of the person's personality, behaviors, and skills.[14] While it's possible that someone who is arrogant is also dishonest or that someone who presents well is organized, it is an unfounded assumption to make the leap without evidence. Having clear criteria and paying close attention to actual behavior during the interview lessens the chance of perceiving something that isn't necessarily there.

Blaming the person versus the circumstance (a.k.a. the fundamental attribution error). If a candidate describes his or her failure to deliver on a project, you might assume he or she lacked the skill to pull it off.[15] But if *you* fail to get something done, you might blame the circumstances—too many insurmountable obstacles. How much blame or credit do we assign to the person versus the circumstances? It depends on whether we're talking about you or someone else. This error is so pervasive and important that its influence on important work-related decisions should not be underestimated, especially in the interview context. Asking for a clear description of the situation and the candidate's thought process can shed light on the complex interplay between situational and personal factors behind what happened.

Stereotyping (a.k.a. the representativeness heuristic). We are all affected by stereotypes; they help make a complex world simpler to understand. They can exert a powerful force on our perceptions and behavior. They are so powerful that our minds often overrule what we know to be statistical facts.[16] When a candidate's description or background fits a stereotype, an interviewer may be prone to judge the candidate by the stereotype rather than the candidate's unique individual qualities. When you feel that a stereotype may be influencing your perceptions, carefully assess whether the behaviors you observed in the candidate validate drawing the conclusions you are making.

Collecting mini-me's (a.k.a. the similar-to-me bias). The basic theory here is that we have the tendency to like and feel more comfortable with individuals whom we see as similar to ourselves. Differences are more difficult to understand and are, therefore, more threatening. It was once thought that this bias was prevalent in the interview, particularly with regard to similar experiences and shared demographics. Recent research suggests that these effects aren't as strong as previously thought. However, it appears that similarities in attitudes may positively influence perceptions.[17]

Blinded by beauty (a.k.a. the attractiveness bias). The attractiveness bias often receives a lot of attention in the media. Despite the number of studies in this area, results are suggestive but not conclusive.[17] The indication is that perceptions of attractive individuals appear reasonably valid but can also be slightly inflated across the board. In other words, an attractive person might indeed be a good planner, negotiator, and strategist but not quite as strong as we perceive him or her to be.

Relatively speaking (a.k.a. the contrast effect). Many individuals and hiring panels fall prey to this illusion. The way the contrast effect works is that after you have seen several mediocre candidates, your perception of an average candidate's skills can be positively inflated.[18] After the candidate is hired, disappointment can set in when the candidate doesn't perform quite as strongly as expected. The best way to combat this is to establish clear standards for evaluating candidates' responses and maintain a consistent approach through all phases of the interview.

Hearsay (a.k.a. the confirmation bias). "I heard this person is a great candidate." Be very mindful of hearsay. Once it has passed your ears, it will create an immediate expectation and an innate desire to search for or pay selective attention to confirming evidence. If the candidate has passed through the initial stages of selection, it's reasonable to expect that he or she comes to the table with some positive skills, but do your best to stay objective and operate with a clean slate. If you feel that others are starting to tell you too much about a candidate, politely ask them to hold on to their comments until after the interview.

Now that you are aware of some common shortcuts and biases, how can you become a more objective interviewer? Interviewing best practices can help you avoid being swayed by your biases. During the interview, focus on gathering data. Observe openly and clearly what is unfolding in the interview. Record information as neutrally as possible. After the interview, explore your emerging impressions and begin to evaluate. Think about this assessment phase as a process of triangulation:

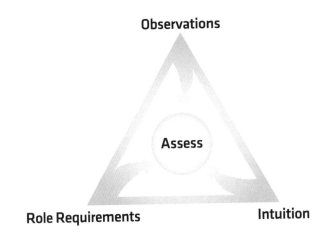

Observations

Assess

Role Requirements

Intuition

Do your observations reconcile with your intuition and the role you are interviewing for? Separating observation from decision making is an effective strategy for staying mindful of the various shortcuts and biases outlined in this chapter.

Using a structured interview such as the Learning From Experience™ Interview Guide can also help you keep biases in check. The structure helps you focus your intuition and fully corroborate that gut feeling. And remember, Learning Agility knows no height, weight, gender, race, class, or global region. Because Learning Agility is evenly distributed throughout the population and around the world, a Learning Agility interview can be conducted in a completely impartial, unbiased manner.

After reading about some of the shortcuts and biases your mind uses when making decisions, you may feel tentative about ever making a decision again. That, in and of itself, would be an irrational bias. So be mindful of these phenomena, but don't let them paralyze you. Intuition is not a bad thing. Selecting the best candidate is an art as well as a science.

Now, all you need to know is what to look for.

Learning Agility

The ability and willingness
to learn from experience, and
subsequently apply that learning to
perform successfully under new
or first-time conditions

Overall Learning Agility

Overall Learning Agility: Knowing What to Do When You Don't Know What to Do

Learning agile people are eager to step out of their comfort zones. They seek out and have more diverse experiences to learn from. They enjoy complex problems and challenges associated with new experiences. And they get more out of their experiences because they have an interest in making sense of them. Ultimately, learning agile people perform better because they incorporate new skills and behaviors into their repertoire.

Examples

Easily learning new functions

Solving problems in a clever or unique way

Thinking strategically

Changing behavior or approach easily

Having wide interests; being highly curious

Dealing well with ambiguity and complexity

Willing to try different approaches

Unwilling to accept the status quo

Recognizing Overall Learning Agility in Others

Learning Agility is not a trait—it's a set of behaviors or tendencies. And Learning Agility is not a construct that is confined to the workplace. In fact, many of the exemplars held up in the *Agile Leader* series are people who have excelled and led in social, political, spiritual, academic, fine arts, and business arenas. Learning agile individuals are a constant work in progress. They view life as a vehicle to explore, invent, reinvent, examine, and question.

Ultimately, Learning Agility is really a methodology or an approach to life. And while some people are more naturally oriented to be learning agile, it can be learned. People can get out of their self-imposed boundaries. Someone who sleepwalks through life can begin to open up their eyes to all kinds of learning and growth and change. People can learn to throw themselves into the deep end. And they can learn to develop a capacity for swimming in the deep end.

The tagline for the *Becoming an Agile Leader* [6] book prompts us to ask a classic question: What do you do when you don't know what to do? When some people encounter a new and unexpected challenge, they might curl up in a ball and hope for the problem to go away, or do what they always do no matter the situation. Other people, those who are more learning agile, actually seek out challenges and problems. They get uncomfortable and restless if they aren't pushed out of their comfort zone often enough.

Learning agile individuals take a fresh look at a given situation; they figure out what is new or different and what is similar to past experiences. Then they sift through their previously acquired lessons and principles and find the ones that apply in the current situation. Finally, they are always making meaning out of things, asking themselves, "What should I be taking away from this?" This constant self-dialogue can take place inside their heads, or it can be moderated by a coach, a colleague, or even an interviewer. Other folks can prompt: "What did you think of that? Why did you approach it that way? What did you take away? What would you do differently?" Whether the insights are self-generated or arrived at through conversation, the learning agile individual is constantly looking for deeper understanding and the opportunity to apply his or her understanding in a useful way.

You'll observe this when you encounter learning agile individuals in your interviews. This constant, purposeful quest for challenging experiences and the never-ending energy put toward making sense of those experiences and applying lessons to the next big challenge. This is why they are rolling stones, works in progress.

"I live life to the full
in a lot of different areas,
so I'm learning all the time."

Sir Richard Branson – Founder, Virgin Group

A Portrait of Overall Learning Agility:
Interviewing Richard Branson

Consider how Sir Richard Branson, a quintessential example of Learning Agility, comes across in the following statements from various interviews. Notice how Branson describes his curiosity and his willingness to try new things. Not only are his ears tuned to hear new ideas, but when an idea resonates with him, he's off and running, ready to tackle it.

> As Branson reflects on his own life experiences, he is quick to note that having dropped out of school at 15, his learning did not stop, rather, he began pursuing an "education of life." He states in his video blog, "I see life as one long university education that I never had—every day I'm learning something new."

From *60 Questions for My 60th year.* Richard Branson. (2010, November).
Retrieved from http://www.virgin.com/richard-branson/blog/

> When Charlie Rose asked Branson how he goes about his learning experience, Branson responded, "I'm open to ideas. The Earth Prize [Virgin Earth Challenge] just came from a discussion with my wife when I said that I just read James Lovelock's latest book and he was saying how hopeless things were, and she turned around and just simply said, 'Man caused the problem; man should be able to solve the problem.'" Reflecting further, Branson said, "I'm a good listener, I think. A lot of my ideas come from other people."

> As the interview drew to a close, Charlie Rose astutely summed Branson up by saying, "But you're curious. The main thing is you're curious."

From "A Conversation with Richard Branson." *Charlie Rose* [Syndicated Public Broadcasting Service (PBS) Television Series]. Charlie Rose. (2008, February 12.)
Retrieved from http://www.charlierose.com/view/interview/8935; minute: 5:04-6:30.

As a leader who has taken his company into multiple industries—from music recording to airlines, railways, beverages, telecommunications, and space travel—Richard Branson is not your average learning agile leader. In the following pages, you'll find descriptions of what to look for and what to listen for as you assess whether a candidate is high, typical, or low in Overall Learning Agility.

*"I've just seen life as
one long learning experience."*

– Sir Richard Branson

High Overall Learning Agility

When a candidate has high Overall Learning Agility, you may hear comments like...

"You can throw something at me and give me zero direction."

"Moving a lot is exciting but hard—I don't ever stay somewhere and become an expert."

"I like that sense of fear when something is new—that feeling in your stomach—I like that."

"I love the complexity of it. No day is the same. There is an ever-changing foundation of how we support the business."

"I know I will be able to figure it out, even if I've never done it before."

Candidates who are high in Overall Learning Agility may share examples in interviews like this one about leading a negotiation between a Native American tribe and a Major League Baseball team.

Situation   I was general counsel for a Major League Baseball team at a time when they were negotiating for land use with a local Native American tribe. You can imagine the business and cultural complexity of those negotiations.

Actions   I asked to lead the negotiation for the firm and requested that everyone take direction from me on this project. I drew upon my reference points from my studies in anthropology. I have a degree in Asian studies, but I also developed an interest in Native American studies and lived on a reservation for several months, many years ago.

Thinking   Missteps could happen so easily, I wanted to make sure our approach was culturally sensitive as well as in the best interests of both parties. I knew that I could draw upon my experiences but that it wouldn't be a direct translation; after all, these were different tribes.

Outcome   We were able to agree on land use, and a new baseball facility was built.

Learnings   Continuous curiosity prevents you from blindly applying what has worked in the past. I learned how to be even more flexible to very different cultural contexts with the tribe and with corporate dealings involving sports executives. I realized that if I kept the end result in sight for both parties, even though it seemed irreconcilable, it opens up the possibilities for a third way that neither party considered before.

Application   Well, interestingly, I've had a couple of failed negotiations since then that have further deepened my understanding of how people's group identity and interests affect their behavior in negotiations. I'm eager to use those learnings in the next deal I'm in charge of.

What about this candidate's example seems to indicate a high level of Overall Learning Agility?

When a candidate has high Overall Learning Agility, you might notice that he or she...

Learns from Experiences

Seizes mistakes and failures as learning opportunities

Processes experiences on a deep level

Actively searches for new ways to apply the lessons learned

Keeps lessons learned consistently at the forefront of his or her thinking

Tends to be philosophical about mistakes and failures

Uses multiple people and sources to learn from

Sees the value in both good and bad experiences; learns from hardships

Learns in real time; assesses problem-solving mistakes and shortcomings for potential lessons

Likes Challenges

Continually strives for growth and improvement

Seeks feedback on a regular basis

Seeks Out the New and the Different

Seeks out new experiences

Surrounds self with diverse people

Is comfortable being a "fish out of water"

Is Adaptable

Is adept in dealing with situations that are dynamic and ambiguous

Demonstrates interpersonal breadth and versatility

Is Compelled to Challenge the Status Quo

Is never complacent or satisfied

Experiments with new approaches

Readily takes risks to make things happen

Watch out for overuse

Too much Overall Learning Agility isn't necessarily a good thing. Overusing Learning Agility can lead to making things too complex, not knowing when to ease up on change efforts, and getting bored easily. People who overuse Learning Agility can be perceived as thriving on chaos, having a limited attention span, and creating instability in an organization.

When a candidate overuses Learning Agility, you may hear comments like...

"I go off on all these tangents that interest me but end up distracting me from what's important."

"I told them to stop the presses because I had another epiphany."

"I get disengaged very quickly when there isn't enough chaos and excitement."

In the rare case of overuse, you might notice that he or she...

Creates a lot of noise in the organization

Takes reckless risks

Experiments too much, to the point
that it does not add value

Brings about change just for the sake of change

Causes others to work harder due to
last-minute changes and ideas

Becomes easily bored

Too frequently takes a contrary
position just for fun

Makes things overly complex when
a simple solution will do

Typical Overall Learning Agility

When a candidate has typical Overall Learning Agility, you may hear comments like...

"I've tried to learn different things over the years that I might be interested in—like mapmaking, biofeedback, etc."

"The most ideal part of my career is continuous learning."

"When I get bored and don't feel challenged, it's a big driver of discomfort. I need to be learning."

"I like someone who is willing to be challenged and willing to challenge me."

"I want to grow. I want to be challenged in different departments."

Candidates who have typical Overall Learning Agility may share examples in interviews like this one about a spiderweb career path.

Situation   I'm building my career at my current company and moving into a department that is not in my core area of expertise.

Actions   I have moved around from business development to marketing and now to product development.

Thinking   I want to explore different areas of the business to expand my understanding. When I'm not an expert, it forces me to try new things and learn new technical areas.

Outcome   It's been challenging but, overall, I've enjoyed it. It's given me a broader understanding of our products, our customers, and how our business works. That being said, I think my ultimate skill and enjoyment are in my original area of business development.

Learnings   It is essential to have the humility to ask my team when I don't know something technical about our area. I realize that there are different ways of operating in each function, and I need to begin almost as an anthropologist might in order to figure out how to be effective.

Application   I am constantly seeing opportunities to learn new things or take up new interests at home and at work. My humility and my stance that there is always something new to learn keep me busy and engaged.

What about this candidate's example suggests a typical amount of Overall Learning Agility?

When a candidate has typical Overall Learning Agility, you might notice that he or she...

Learns from Experiences

Looks to the lessons of the past, but may be less interested in reviewing personal mistakes and shortcomings

Has made role changes and can extract insights from these experiences when prompted

Likes Challenges

Seeks out new challenges and wants to embark on new journeys; gets fascinated with new things to do

Seeks Out the New and the Different

Is interested in the new and different, and can open self up to new possibilities

Approaches situations with an open mind

Is willing to take initiative and experiment with trying something new

Is Adaptable

Displays flexibility in taking on different roles,
and alters behaviors to suit various situations

Is willing to venture outside of comfort zone and deal
with moderate levels of complexity and ambiguity

Works through shades of gray by enlisting support and
engagement of others; likes it when others can bring
overall clarity on what is required to be delivered

Is accepting of the ambiguity and complexity
inherent in most business situations

Is Compelled to Challenge the Status Quo

Is motivated to come up with new ideas and
ways to approach everyday situations

Low Overall Learning Agility

**When a candidate has low Overall Learning Agility,
you may hear comments like...**

"I haven't done this before—
we need someone who has."

"Unless I know I'm right,
I'm not comfortable."

"I understand I need to get
out of my comfort zone.
I just don't want to."

"There's a lot that
I hate to do."

Candidates who are low in Overall Learning Agility may share examples in interviews like this one about a lawsuit.

Situation   Eight months ago, this guy called and said he was going to sue our company because an ad we created looked like something he had posted online.

Actions   I called legal, and they wanted me to solve it without going to litigation. I tried to reason with the guy, but he was trying to get me to do business with him and threatening to sue at the same time.

Thinking   I like to take care of things so my boss doesn't have to deal with it. I don't want to get her involved unless I have to.

Outcome   The guy sent our CEO a letter explaining the situation and complaining about me. My boss and the CEO were taken off guard because they didn't know everything about the whole situation.

Learnings   This was kind of a one-off. There are crazy, unreasonable people out there. I'm not sure you can prepare for that.

Application   I haven't had to deal with anybody like that since then.

What do you notice about this example that indicates a low level of Overall Learning Agility?

When a candidate has low Overall Learning Agility, you might notice that he or she...

Learns from Experiences

Is unable to think in broad-enough terms to apply lessons from one experience to a different, unrelated experience

May go through experiences without distilling them adequately

Tends to be more declarative than inquisitive

Shows no pattern of learning new things from experiences

Has a distorted view of self

Likes Challenges

Gets upset and discouraged when experiencing setbacks

Is not sure how to identify or deploy his or her strengths and weaknesses

Seeks Out the New and the Different

Needs to seek opportunities for challenge and personal growth —still somewhat limited in breadth and diversity of experiences

Seeks out the same types of jobs and experiences

Has difficulty performing well in first-time and challenging situations

Is Adaptable

Uses fewer problem-solving strategies

Does not adjust quickly in the face of feedback

Has difficulty dealing with ambiguous situations

Is Compelled to Challenge the Status Quo

Avoids uncertainty; is comfortable
with the way things are

Focuses too much on knowing the right
answer and being self-reliant

As you assess Overall Learning Agility, keep in mind that while it's helpful to consider the candidate's skill level in the different factors, Overall Learning Agility is greater than the sum of its parts. There is a certain "X factor" that both encompasses all of the factors and is an additive quality to a person's Learning Agility.

One way to think about it is whether the candidate appears to be an active learner. Compared to traditional learners or more passive learners, active or agile learners are energized by challenges, tend to experiment, take initiative, are always curious, take risks, and are incredibly resourceful. You might describe them as awake or conscious of the world around them, constantly processing and making sense of what they are experiencing, and ready to take new approaches to new challenges. In this sense, agile learners embody an overarching quality of active learning that includes, but also goes beyond, any of the specific Learning Agility factors.

"Every day I'm learning something new."

– Sir Richard Branson

Learning Agility Factor

The degree to which an individual has personal insight, clearly understands their own strengths and weaknesses, is free of blind spots, and uses this knowledge to perform effectively

Self-Awareness

Seeking Personal Insight

Self-Awareness:
Seeking Personal Insight

To be self-aware is to know yourself, to understand your strengths and limitations. It means having a tendency to seek feedback and act on it. Being introspective about mistakes and failures in order to learn from them. And staying on the lookout for new experiences to help refine or learn new skills. Internal reflection enables the expression of thoughts, feelings, and opinions with candor.

Examples

Being honest with yourself about strengths and weaknesses

Asking for feedback

Taking constructive feedback to heart and acting on it

Knowing why you're feeling a certain way

Willing to admit mistakes but not dwell on them

Looking for new personal insights

Recognizing Self-Awareness in Others

When you find yourself across the table from someone who is self-aware, you will notice that the conversation is relaxed and easy. Self-aware people don't have anything to hide. Because of this, they come across as frank and authentic. In other words, what you see is what you get.

If you interview regularly, it's generally easy to tell when people are trying to tell you what they think you want to hear and be who they think you want them to be. Changing themselves like chameleons takes a lot of effort, and they can't keep it up.

On the other hand, self-aware people recognize that they are a work in progress. They will likely engage with you, actively reflecting in the moment, seeking insight into their thoughts and actions. The pattern of behavior you will see is someone who is committed to a cycle of evaluation and inquiry: What did I do? What could I do differently? What impact did I have on people and on the situation? How might this have been seen? How might I change or adjust next time?

When you ask self-aware individuals "Why did you approach the situation the way that you did?" you will see evidence that they were conscious of the alternatives, sought feedback, and thoughtfully selected their approach. When asked to evaluate how successful their approach was, self-aware people take a more detached, philosophical approach. They accept responsibility for their actions, but stop short of beating themselves up and dwelling on missteps.

People who are self-aware strive toward a mindful state of being—maintaining a neutral, nonjudgmental awareness of their emotions and experiences which leads toward more conscious control of choices and responses. While mindfulness is not a new concept, its recent surge in popularity can be traced to its purported benefits: more flexibility, improved concentration, decreased stress, enhanced compassion, and a calm state of mind.

Most of us need a coach or a colleague to help us think things through, become aware of our helpful and not-so-helpful behaviors, accept our strengths and weaknesses, and motivate us to take action. Self-aware individuals fulfill the coaching role for themselves. In their responses, you'll hear a proactive, self-sourced approach to self-improvement. The insight comes from their own reflection. At the same time, they know when they need help gaining insight, so they seek feedback and input from people around them.

Self-Awareness and People Agility are two factors that are closely linked to emotional intelligence. You will often note that people who are higher in one tend to be higher in the other.

"Without willing it, I had gone from being ignorant of being ignorant to being aware of being aware."

Maya Angelou – American poet, author, civil rights activist

A Portrait of Self-Awareness:
Interviewing Maya Angelou

Maya Angelou is an exemplar of Self-Awareness. See if you can recognize some of the qualities of her Self-Awareness by hearing what she says in her writings and her conversations.

In *I Know Why the Caged Bird Sings*, the first of her six autobiographies, Angelou shares an experience of awakening. She took a semester off from high school to work in the real world, and returned to school feeling older and wiser. She writes,

"Without willing it, I had gone from being ignorant of being ignorant to being aware of being aware. And the worst part of my awareness was that I didn't know what I was aware of. I knew I knew very little, but I was certain that the things I had yet to learn wouldn't be taught to me at George Washington High School."

From *I Know Why the Caged Bird Sings*. Maya Angelou. (1969). New York, NY: Random House.

Upon returning home from a working engagement in Europe, Angelou was distressed by what her absence had done to her son. She recalls that even as she slipped into numbness and depression, "I was aware I was not acting like the old Maya..."

From *Singin' and Swingin' and Gettin' Merry Like Christmas*. Maya Angelou. (1976). New York, NY: Random House.

When asked in an interview if she considered herself to be wise, Angelou responded, "Well, I'm en route. I am certainly on the road."

From "Oprah Talks to Maya Angelou." [Interview]. (2000, December). *O, The Oprah Magazine*. Retrieved from http://www.oprah.com/omagazine/Oprah-Interviews-Maya-Angelou/3#ixzz20Qf2IQfi

Maya Angelou knows herself. She pays attention. She seeks wisdom. She reflects on her life, her experiences, and who she is. She's written six autobiographies! But remember, while Angelou is exceptionally high in self-awareness, you are likely to find these behaviors to varying degrees in the people you interview. When you interview candidates, how will you know whether you are observing high, typical, or low Self-Awareness? The following pages highlight what qualities to look for as well as what to listen for. If you are interested in honing your ability to assess Self-Awareness, take a look at the examples of high-, typical-, and low-scoring individuals and how their Self-Awareness comes through in their comments and stories. These examples came from actual interviews conducted by the authors using the Learning From Experience™ Interview Guide. We share them here to provide some orientation and a baseline that will help you evaluate candidates you interview.

"Just listening to you now,
I'm thinking 'What is it about Maya?'
I think it's that you know yourself."

– Oprah Winfrey
(speaking to Maya Angelou - *O Magazine*, Dec. 2000)

High Self-Awareness

When a candidate has high Self-Awareness, you may hear comments like...

"I am definitely contemplative."

"Asking for feedback and being aware of my issues in dealing with people and relationships is helping. Now I think through the person that I'm talking to and where they're coming from."

"(The best boss I ever had) really gave me clear and immediate feedback."

High Self-Awareness candidates may offer examples in interviews like this one about the need to upskill.

Situation   When I started my business development job, I knew my business acumen was not strong enough. I shared with my manager that I was not feeling completely confident.

Actions   I did a mini needs assessment on myself. Then I scoured our company's learning and development site to see what online finance courses I could take. I also found an internal mentor to help me understand commercial levers, different metrics, and how to read certain reports.

Thinking   When I feel a lack of confidence, it's not always due to a lack of knowledge or a lack of understanding, so I need to locate the root cause and what will help. In this case, education was the key.

Outcome   My confidence grew, I was able to add value to my team, and my performance improved.

Learnings   It's so important to be humble enough to acknowledge when you don't know something. If I admit that to myself, then I can be resourceful, take initiative, and use my curiosity to learn what I need to learn.

Application   In subsequent roles, I have tried to reflect and ask myself the right questions. I have sought out coaching, training, and feedback as much as possible. I've even gone through some training to become a coach to others.

What about this candidate's example seems to indicate a high level of Self-Awareness?

When a candidate has high Self-Awareness, you might notice that he or she...

Personal Learner

Shows strong commitment to learning and self-improvement

Seeks to continually learn and refine his or her approach

Feedback Oriented

Seeks and is responsive to coaching and suggestions for how to further improve performance

Views criticism as helpful

Reflective

Reflects on and takes lessons from mistakes and failures

Reviews situations and contemplates what he or she could have done differently

Engages in active reflection in an effort to acquire deeper insight and learning

Emotion Management

Stays composed, even while others get emotional

Weighs emotions when making decisions

Self-Knowledge

Demonstrates above-average self-insight

Admits to mistakes and shortcomings

Is very open and forthcoming

Has a good sense of self and is realistic
regarding strengths and needs

Watch out for overuse

Too much Self-Awareness isn't necessarily a good thing. When Self-Awareness goes into overdrive, it can lead to a debilitating self-consciousness or being overly critical of oneself. As a result, someone who overuses Self-Awareness may be perceived as lacking confidence and taking tentative steps when bold action is needed.

When a candidate overuses Self-Awareness, you may hear comments like...

"I'm never very good at..."

"I just can't stop thinking about how I could have approached that interaction differently."

"I'm not ready to move forward until I hear everyone's feedback."

In the rare case of overuse, you might notice that he or she...

Solicits feedback indiscriminately
and seemingly without purpose

Becomes dependent on feedback to the
point that no moves are made without it

Spends too much time reflecting on
the past and hesitates to move on

Is self-critical to the point of risking
credibility and appearing insecure

Is overly open, assertive, and
candid about shortcomings

Typical Self-Awareness

When a candidate has typical Self-Awareness, you may hear comments like...

"For me, it's all about incremental improvement. How we can learn from our mistakes."

"I've gotten feedback in the past about needing to 'rein it in' and stay grounded."

"Perhaps I could have done that differently."

Candidates with typical Self-Awareness may offer examples in interviews like this one, where taking feedback too personally led to a rocky start.

Situation   When our SVP started years ago, we didn't know how he wanted things to work. He didn't think I was doing the right thing. He didn't think I was successful. It was a rocky six months.

Actions   I worked together with my boss to understand what he was looking for—we stumbled and fell, and then walked and fell, and then finally hit the ground running. Eventually, I realized that he had higher expectations of me, and I had to rise to that. At first, I was very closed off to the idea that I wasn't doing a good job. In the past, I had always been told that I was doing a good job. I really personalized it. I like being an A student. I made him the bad guy.

Thinking   When I look back, I was pretty immature in my feelings about it. I didn't think, "This is a business, and he has business needs that I'm not meeting." I had to change my attitude and work toward what he wanted.

Outcome   In the end, when I was promoted, he was one of my biggest champions.

Learnings   I realized I needed to see things from his perspective. Accepting his feedback as valid, rather than being a victim to it, allowed me to move on and do my job better.

Application The older I get, the more agile I am at navigating through change—which is strange—but now I more readily admit, "I get it, I'm going to have to transform a little bit."

What about this candidate's example suggests a typical amount of Self-Awareness?

When a candidate has typical Self-Awareness, you might notice that he or she...

Personal Learner

Seeks mentors for areas that he or she needs to grow in or lacks confidence in

Feedback Oriented

Has to build up the courage to ask for feedback from others

Is learning to accept criticism

Is learning not to personalize criticism

Reflective

Takes time for reflection and introspection

Has some strong feelings beneath the surface, but is able to control the expression of those feelings

Is insightful about mistakes, tries to wrest meaning from failures, and is continuing to better understand himself or herself

Emotion Management

Struggles to stay composed, even while others get emotional

Allows emotions to drive some decisions

Self-Knowledge

Knows personal strengths and weaknesses, for the most part

Is sensitive to the impact he or she has on other people

Demonstrates appropriate openness

Is cautious, but generally approaches others in a
transparent and straightforward manner

Relies on other people's expertise when it is an
area of weakness for him or her

Low Self-Awareness

When a candidate has low Self-Awareness, you may hear comments like...

"It's not my fault; you're the one who..."

"I just lost it, I couldn't help it."

"Let me give you some feedback."

Candidates who are low in Self-Awareness may offer examples in interviews in which blame and defensiveness become barriers in working relationships.

Situation   When I first started here, I had a production partner with a tough personality—pretty competitive and quick to assume the worst. Everyone else was very respectful, but not her.

Actions   When she would come at me with accusations, I would lose my composure and go back at her. When she pushed my buttons, she made herself look bad, but I also made myself look bad.

Thinking   It's something that's in my personality to engage in that way.

Outcome   My boss pulled me aside and said, "I know she's tough, but you have to rise above it." And I wanted to say, "But she…" and blame her for the dynamic. But my boss had just told me that I needed to stay composed.

Learnings   You have to remove yourself when it gets like that if you can't respond in a calm way. I have a lot of passion in me, and I have to rise above it and keep myself out of it.

Application   I'm not sure I've done a very good job of reforming myself on this front. I know how I should engage, in theory, but my passion and emotion continue to drive my reactions.

What do you notice about this example that indicates a low level of Self-Awareness?

When a candidate has low Self-Awareness, you might notice that he or she...

Personal Learner

Is satisfied with current portfolio of skills, and is less interested in pursuing development opportunities

Feedback Oriented

Gets defensive and blames others

Readily gives feedback and makes recommendations, but does not apply advice to self or own team

Is not interested in making changes based on feedback

Reflective

Does not manage emotions; shows frustration, condescension, annoyance, and impatience

Approaches many issues with passion and intensity; occasionally needs to curb emotions

Shows limited self-reflection; would benefit from more inner reflection

Emotion Management

Loses composure in tense or emotional situations

Is often captive to own emotions; unable to
maintain perspective

Self-Knowledge

Is not sure why he or she hasn't considered other approaches

Is very comfortable in own skin, but actual self-awareness
is somewhat beneath the surface

Could have stronger awareness of the impact he or she has

Sees the value in being vulnerable and transparent,
but still gaining full comfort with this

Is sometimes slow to pick up on the unwritten rules
and subtle nuances of social situations

To become better at assessing Self-Awareness, it helps to work on your own Self-Awareness. As you reflect on situations that candidates shared with you in the course of the Learning Agility interview, consider how you would have responded in a similar situation and why. Take the opportunity of evaluating others' Self-Awareness to evaluate and improve your own. For more ideas, check out *Becoming an Agile Leader*.

Once you've assessed the level of Self-Awareness the candidate has, put that in context of the role he or she is interviewing for. What part does Self-Awareness play in that role? Is it a position that requires thoughtful response, learning from mistakes, continuous feedback? If so, Self-Awareness will be mission critical.

"You have to get to a very quiet place inside yourself.
And that doesn't mean that you can't have noise outside.
I know some people who put jazz on, loudly, to write.
I think each writer has her or his secret path to the muse."

– Maya Angelou

Learning Agility Factor

The extent to which an individual embraces complexity, examines problems in unique and unusual ways, is inquisitive, and can make fresh connections between different concepts

Mental Agility

Making Fresh Connections

Mental Agility:
Making Fresh Connections

To be mentally agile is to be drawn toward newness and complexity. It is the ability to be mentally quick, to delve deeply and thoroughly analyze problems, and to find parallels and contrasts that inform fresh thinking. Mental Agility is exemplified in a curious, inquisitive, and analytical nature in the search for meaning.

Examples

Approaching the world with curiosity

Making connections that prove difficult for others

Searching for deeper meaning

Simplifying the complex so others can also grasp it

Solving problems by applying deep analysis
and fresh perspective

Helping others think things through

Seeing many parts of something while
simultaneously divining its essence

Recognizing Mental Agility in Others

When it comes to assessing Mental Agility, there are two primary things to look for in a candidate: nimbleness of thought when presented with a problem situation and the variety of approaches at the candidate's disposal.

Mentally agile people have numerous problem-solving tools on their tool belt. When a new problem lands on their desk, they're able to deftly examine the nature of the problem and apply the right tools—both in the discovery phase and in crafting a solution.

There are some people who can really analyze and solve problems, but they have a default process. With any problem they encounter, they choose to take the same approach. They dissect it in the same step-by-step manner, fit it into their preexisting categories, and try to find the right answer. For some situations their default approach works, for some it does not.

You may have heard the saying, "When all you have is a hammer, everything looks like a nail." People lower in Mental Agility overrely on one or two tools, or may only have one or two tools. People higher in Mental Agility have a collection of tools, they're at some level of mastery in using each of them, and they instinctively know which one to reach for, given the particular demands of the situation.

When tackling a problem, people who are more mentally agile call upon a wide variety of resources and seek multiple points of view. They often intuit when they are not seeing the whole story and are quick to think critically about the problem. They consider other problems that would help them deal with the problem in front of them. They make connections. They walk around the problem, look at it from all angles, scan the horizon, get above it, work through it, and go to other areas outside their expertise. You can tell that they are not just relying on their default approach. It's almost as if they are thinking in 3-D.

"To raise new questions,
new possibilities, to regard
old problems from a new angle,
requires creative imagination and
marks real advance in science."

Albert Einstein – German-born American physicist and Nobel Prize winner

A Portrait of Mental Agility:
Interviewing Albert Einstein

The following interview contains excerpts from a simulated interview with Albert Einstein. The interview was compiled by Dr. Dan Albert for *Science Careers Blog* (Albert, 2011). These statements highlight how Einstein, an archetype of Mental Agility, reflects on intellectual pursuits.

Question What are the results of a scientific career that makes it worthwhile and exciting?

Einstein It is not the *result* of scientific research that ennobles humans and enriches their nature, but the *struggle to understand* while performing creative and open-minded intellectual work. It is my inner conviction that the development of science seeks in the main to satisfy the longing for pure knowledge.

Question But I would have thought it's the new knowledge one brings to light—the discoveries—that make a science career worthwhile?

Einstein The word "discovery" in itself is regrettable. For discovery is equivalent to becoming aware of a thing which is already formed; this links up with proof, which no longer bears the character of "discovery" but, in the final analysis, of the means that leads to discovery....Discovery is really not a creative act.

Question What advice would you give for picking the best school for one's scientific training?

Einstein The school should always have as its aim that the young person leave it as a harmonious personality, not as a specialist. Otherwise, he—with his specialized knowledge—more closely resembles a well-trained dog than a harmoniously developed person.

Question And what would you look for in a teacher?

Einstein The most valuable thing a teacher can impart to children is not knowledge and understanding per se but a longing for knowledge and understanding, and an appreciation for intellectual values, whether they be artistic, scientific, or moral. It is the supreme art of the teacher to awaken joy in creative expression and knowledge. Most teachers waste their time by asking questions that are intended to discover what a pupil does not know, whereas the true art of questioning is to discover what the pupil does know or is capable of knowing.

Question And what should the attitude of the student be?

Einstein It is not so very important for a person to learn facts. For that he does not really need a college. He can learn them from books. The value of an education in a liberal arts college is not learning of many facts, but the training of the mind to think something that cannot be learned from textbooks.

Used with permission. From "An Interview with Albert Einstein on Science Careers." *Science Careers Blog*. Dan Albert. (2011, January 14). Retrieved from http://blogs.sciencemag.org/sciencecareers/2011/01/an-interview-wi.html

Albert Einstein is known for being extremely intelligent, but here the emphasis is his Mental Agility. His ability and desire to be creative and think differently about problems. The interview highlights Einstein's disdain for the term *discovery* and highlights his preference for *creativity*. He underscores education's role in fostering students' curiosity and broad thinking. The focus on questioning, problem solving, and the ability to "think something that cannot be learned from textbooks" gets to the essence of Mental Agility. In the following pages, you will see examples of individuals who are high, typical, and low in Mental Agility. Use the behaviors and qualities to help you assess Mental Agility in candidates you interview.

*"The value of an education
in a liberal arts college
is not learning of many facts,
but the training of the mind
to think something that
cannot be learned from textbooks."*

– Albert Einstein

High Mental Agility

**When a candidate has high Mental Agility,
you may hear comments like...**

"I love helping people
discover an answer to the
problem. I love to crack
the code on stuff."

"I want to figure out
different connections
—I don't think about
it as problem solving."

"I generally
bring a different
answer/suggestion
than the rest of the group
—I have an ability to
see possibilities."

Candidates high in Mental Agility may offer examples in interviews like this one about the problem solving involved in building a pier.

Situation   Our company (steel manufacturer) was commissioned to supply the steel framework for a pier in New York City's harbor that would permanently house an aircraft carrier. This had never been done before. There were numerous parties involved, and no one knew the best way to solve it. To complicate things, the way we manufactured our steel did not fit the spec for this pier that needed to be three football fields long.

Actions   I went into full fact-finding and exploration mode with all parties involved. I worked with the customer (the Port Authority) to get a grasp of the myriad of stakeholder needs that had to be considered and balanced. I worked with our engineers to change the manufacturing process to design custom girders for the project. I had to consult with my bosses to make sure that we wouldn't undermine the profitability of the project.

Thinking   I realized right away that this was not merely a technical problem. We had to solve half-a-dozen problems to get a solution to the main problem. Everyone was stumped. Everyone involved had to do something different from normal protocol to make it work—it wasn't a normal situation. I made it my role to navigate and coordinate between everyone.

Outcome   I brought all the parties into alignment to agree on the solution so that we could execute. We met our project milestones.

Learnings   I realized that sometimes the best solution overall is not the optimal solution for any one party. Not that everyone has to compromise, but everyone needs to deviate from the normal or preferred way of doing things. Solving a problem of this complexity requires patience, attentiveness, and constantly making the rounds with different stakeholders.

Application I've limbered up a muscle, and I'm adeptly able to navigate multiple stakeholders to solve a problem. I stretched skills so far that those situations come very easily now.

What about this candidate's example seems to indicate a high level of Mental Agility?

When a candidate has high Mental Agility, you might notice that he or she...

Inquisitive

Demonstrates strong intellectual curiosity and is intrigued by cutting-edge ideas

Demonstrates a healthy skepticism and critical-thinking skills; is willing to challenge conventional wisdom

Is eager to explore diverse and novel ideas

Thinks in possibility; is open-minded, imaginative, and willing to take novel approaches

Broad Scanner

Seeks to broaden horizons by tackling new and complex problems

Cleverly frames a problem by looking at the broader context, and viewing it from a number of different angles

Uses insightful analogies and metaphors

Connector

Is an integrative thinker—effectively gathers and synthesizes large amounts of data, and integrates diverse streams of information

Is quick to make non-obvious connections, including those that might not be apparent to others

Translates abstract ideas into workable action steps

Essence

Is able to discern which variables are important versus those that are more trivial

Gets at root causes

Complexity

Considers the consequences, broader implications, and possible outcomes; thinks through a problem forwards and backwards

Has learned to apply common principles to specific situations through tweaking and adaptation

Has a sharp eye for details and nuances; dives deep into problems, but is generally mindful of not getting immersed for too long

Manages Uncertainty

Thrives when venturing outside of comfort zone and dealing with high levels of complexity and ambiguity

Balances analysis and intuition, knowledge and insight, quickness and thoroughness, openness and decisiveness

Watch out for overuse

Too much Mental Agility isn't necessarily a good thing. Overusing Mental Agility can lead to analysis paralysis or being dismissive of simple, elegant solutions. People who overuse Mental Agility may be perceived as impractical, or valuing intellectual exercise more than solving business problems.

When a candidate overuses Mental Agility, you may hear comments like...

"I'm constantly looking for new ways to solve a problem—I don't pay much attention to what has worked in the past."

"I have a hard time getting people to keep up with my line of thinking."

"My instinct is that problems are always more complex than they appear."

In the rare case of overuse, you might notice that he or she...

Has a tendency to overanalyze and overcomplexify

Processes new information too quickly, forms impressions prematurely, and makes snap judgments

May not fully appreciate tried-and-true solutions in searching for the new and different

Is ahead of others' thinking; needs to be more attentive to bringing others around to the same understanding

Typical Mental Agility

**When a candidate has typical Mental Agility,
you may hear comments like...**

"I like to ask questions,
so I don't mind when I don't
understand something."

"I hear something
and I want to solve it
right away. So I have
to be careful not to
jump to solutions
too quickly."

"I'm very interested in
taking a multi-disciplinary
approach."

When candidates are typical in Mental Agility, you may hear examples in interviews like this one about being resourceful and developing a "guerilla business strategy."

Situation We needed to build a licensing partnership to elevate our brand. The tough part was how to pitch the idea to a big brand and get them to listen. Our conventional approach of building a business plan first wasn't going to work because this was all about who you know.

Actions I used my network and called a guy who had a friend who worked at the brand I was targeting for this partnership. When that didn't work, I went to the same conferences and, basically, stalked this person. When I approached her, I told her, "I think I can help you make money."

Thinking This business is all about relationships. I needed to get face-to-face and make the introduction.

Outcome We're on the brink of testing something in key markets.

Learnings I learned that there was no plan or process or PowerPoint deck or calendar—I just needed a guerilla business strategy. It completely unlocked the business. I just have to do whatever it takes to get the partnership established.

Application Since then, I've taken on a couple of new growth strategies for the business, and I am approaching it not only from a business plan standpoint but also with a focus on relationships.

What about this candidate's example suggests a typical amount of Mental Agility?

When a candidate has typical Mental Agility, you might notice that he or she...

Inquisitive

Is appropriately skeptical; doesn't take things at face value

Typically avoids getting stuck on a single solution; regroups and tries alternative tactics when initial efforts don't meet with success

Is sometimes willing to branch out and try something bold and different

Broad Scanner

Seeks new information; periodically refreshes thinking and makes adjustments to his or her approach

Tries to flesh out a more complete, multi-dimensional view of a problem, rather than seeing it as black and white

Connector

Sees connectivity below surface features of a situation or a problem

Is capable of connecting disparate dots before arriving at final conclusions

Is great at generating new ideas, but may hesitate to figure out how to actually implement them

Essence

Looks beyond surface issues and gets to root causes

Sometimes seizes upon key elements that others may overlook

Keeps the common purpose and context in mind, and fashions
effective solutions that meet the objectives

Complexity

Patiently peels back the layers of a problem to reach a workable
solution, even where there are no precedents

Gives consideration to consequences and implications,
and lets those drive the strategy and actions

Manages Uncertainty

Leaves room for unexpected or surprising possibilities

Balances analysis with intuition and allows evidence to
support or refute hunches

Low Mental Agility

When a candidate has low Mental Agility, you may hear comments like...

"I did exactly what was needed, exactly what was asked for."

"There was no other way to do it."

"That idea was just not practical."

"I got so focused on the problem and my solution, I didn't pay attention to new and emerging information."

Candidates who are low in Mental Agility may share examples in interviews that highlight the lack of options for solving a problem.

Situation   I worked with a challenging client on a large technology implementation project. She didn't know what she was doing, which made her nervous and indecisive. She asked for a myriad of examples and information before she felt comfortable moving ahead.

Actions   I felt that I had to push her to trust me—she was always questioning, always tentative and skeptical. One time, I even brought a senior leader in on a call to help me build my credibility with her. I gave her as much information as possible because there was no other approach.

Thinking   I did exactly what she said she needed. There was no other way to do it.

Outcome   She trusts me more now and trusts my recommendations.

Learnings   I learned that I have to have patience. I need to get ahead of clients' nervousness and overload them with information.

Application   Since then, after every meeting, I send a summary on project status and decisions. I think it makes nervous people feel heard.

What do you notice about this example that indicates a low level of Mental Agility?

When a candidate has low Mental Agility, you might notice that he or she...

Inquisitive

Can be overreliant on practical, analytical approach at the expense of creative, intuitive methods

Is not likely to experiment with new techniques

Is somewhat dogmatic in his or her approach, but willing to rethink when prompted

May be overly focused on what other people think—at times merely executes others' ideas, at times may be paralyzed by others' opinions of his or her own ideas

Broad Scanner

Is less open to divergent points of view, new information, and new possibilities

Struggles to integrate the information he or she gathers

Goes to the same limited resources to solve problems

Connector

Reaches strong conclusions too quickly

Could sometimes show more spontaneity and intuition

Would benefit from spending more time exploring options and surfacing beliefs

Essence

Can describe the parts of a problem or situation but not the underlying causes that require more scrutiny to gain a deeper understanding

Tends to overanalyze and has a preference for precise understanding, stifling openness to reevaluation of options

Complexity

Tends to take the same favored approach to solving problems

Is inconsistent in the ability to move between the big picture and the details; may focus on one at the cost of the other

Becomes overwhelmed when problem is complicated; seeks to simplify

Manages Uncertainty

Is focused on a right way of doing things

Prefers what has worked in the past, rather than looking for new tactics

Is not comfortable when relying on assumptions or intuition; prefers facts

Takes longer to let highly abstract issues sink in; prefers the concrete

To become better at assessing Mental Agility, it helps to work on your own Mental Agility. As you reflect on situations that candidates shared with you in the course of the Learning Agility interview, consider how you would have responded in a similar situation and why. Take the opportunity of evaluating others' Mental Agility to evaluate and improve your own. For more ideas, check out *Becoming an Agile Leader*.

Once you've assessed the level of Mental Agility the candidate has, put that in context of the role he or she is interviewing for. What part does Mental Agility play in that role? Is it a position that requires dealing with complex problems, finding creative solutions, or making new connections? If so, Mental Agility will be mission critical.

"The most valuable thing a teacher can impart to children is not knowledge and understanding per se but a longing for knowledge and understanding, and an appreciation for intellectual values, whether they be artistic, scientific, or moral."

– Albert Einstein

Learning Agility Factor

The degree to which one is
open-minded toward others, enjoys
interacting with a diversity of people,
understands their unique strengths,
interests, and limitations, and uses
them effectively to accomplish
organizational goals

People Agility

Bringing Out the Best in Others

People Agility:
Bringing Out the Best in Others

People Agility is the ability to relate well to others—taking a flexible approach, depending on the person or the situation. People agile individuals listen, understand, and empathize with others. Open-minded toward people and situations, they are willing to shift their perspective or position. They bring out the best in others and can get things done through other people. And, depending on the situation, they exhibit appropriate lightheartedness.

Examples

Relating well to all kinds of people

Getting things done through others

Navigating both interpersonal
and political dynamics

Listening and understanding
others' points of view

Adjusting style and approach
for different people

Dealing with conflict in a way
that doesn't burn bridges

Recognizing People Agility in Others

There are two elements to listen for when interviewing for People Agility—the ability to read and adjust to other people (individuals and groups) and the ability to read and adjust to the situation. An initial scan of the people and the situation can establish a baseline that guides one's approach, but situations and people are not static. Due to the constant reciprocal nature of interactions, those high in People Agility are constantly monitoring and recalibrating.

You'll often find that people who are higher in People Agility tend to be higher in Self-Awareness. People agile individuals are self-monitoring, keenly aware of the situation, what needs to be done, and where they are in relation to it. And it's not about being all things to all people; there is an element of authenticity. The individuals most effective in the area of People Agility are aware of their own default preferences—what their tendencies are in certain situations. Their awareness of this allows for a modification even before an encounter begins.

Candidates high in People Agility will read and adjust to the Learning Agility interview in real time. They will pick up quickly on the nature of the questioning and adapt themselves to the situation. The first question is often a test-drive, but when they get a sense of what's happening, they will understand immediately that it's in their best interest to tell it like it is. People agile candidates will take the time to dig deep and show you who they are. They sense that embellishment and spin are not going to help, that being themselves will meet the interviewer's objective of making the best decision based on who they are and what the role requires.

For candidates who are high in People Agility, you will notice that the experiences they share in the interview contain rich, vivid descriptions of the people and the setting. Because they have an author's eye for detail, their stories will come to life so that you almost feel as if you were there. Their emotional intelligence in the moment and their ability to decode the interpersonal dynamics upon reflection contribute to the engaging way they retell the experience. And, because they've worked to see the situation from multiple points of view, they often let a story unfold with a nuanced complexity that allows for ambiguity and contradictions. It's less "just the facts" and more "director's commentary."

For candidates who overuse People Agility, you'll notice that they focus so much on calibration that their baseline evaporates, and they become chameleon-like in their behavior—no longer grounded in who they are. This can lead to overly political behavior or an outsized focus on collaboration at the expense of getting things done.

"If you want the cooperation
of humans around you,
you must make them
feel they are important
– and you do that by
being genuine and humble."

Nelson Mandela – Former South African president

A Portrait of People Agility:
Interviewing Nelson Mandela

Nelson Mandela is an archetype of People Agility. His ability to read others, build rapport with people who opposed him, and become a force of reconciliation are just a few of the reasons Mandela is highly people agile. In the following conversation with Richard Stengel about Mandela's speech-making style, see if you can hear evidence of People Agility in his responses.

Stengel Sometimes people do criticize you for not being a more rousing speaker.

Mandela Well, in a climate of this nature, when we are trying to reach a settlement through negotiations you don't want rabble-rousing speeches. You want to discuss problems with people soberly, because the people would like to know how you behave or how you express yourself, and then they can have an idea of how you are handling important issues in the course of those negotiations. The masses like to see somebody who is responsible and who speaks in a responsible manner. They like that, and so I avoid rabble-rousing speech. I don't want to incite the crowd. I want the crowd to understand what we are doing and I want to infuse a spirit of reconciliation to them.

Stengel Would you say your speaking style is different now than in the old days before you went to prison?

Mandela Well, I have mellowed, very definitely, and as a young man, you know, I was very radical and using high-flown language, and fighting everybody. But now, you know, one has to lead and...a rabble-rousing speech therefore is not appropriate.

Used with permission. From *Conversations with Myself*. Nelson Mandela. (2010, pp. 325–326). New York, NY: Farrar, Straus and Giroux.

Nelson Mandela knows how to bring out the best in other people. He sees a way through conflict and calls upon shared humanity to reconcile differences. Mandela is an inspiring model of People Agility. Most people possess a more moderate level of People Agility. When you interview candidates, how will you know whether you are observing high, typical, or low People Agility? Review the following pages to see what qualities to look for as well as what to listen for as you conduct a Learning Agility interview. If you are interested in honing your ability to assess People Agility, take a look at the examples of high-, typical-, and low-scoring individuals. These examples came from actual interviews conducted by the authors using the Learning From Experience™ Interview Guide. We share them here to provide some orientation and a baseline that will help you evaluate candidates you interview.

"I learned to have the patience to listen when people put forward their views, even if I think those views are wrong. You can't reach a just decision in a dispute unless you listen to both sides, ask questions, and view the evidence placed before you."

– Nelson Mandela

High People Agility

When a candidate has high People Agility, you may hear comments like…

"I have matured in my leadership style—I've learned to tap what makes others tick and have been much more successful in that. In the past, during the first 15 years of my career, I was much more of a 'jump on the train' kind of guy."

"I am a calm presence—people come to me during difficult times."

"I'm not a bull in a china shop— not one to 'jolt' other people."

"I'm not afraid of taking risks, but when you have to make decisions that affect others, it's a concern."

"I will deliberately determine when the situation calls for a change or departure in my style."

When candidates are high in People Agility, you may hear examples in interviews like this one about a family cabin.

Situation   When my uncle passed away unexpectedly, the fate of the family cabin was thrown up in the air. His will did not stipulate ownership clearly, and a family dispute erupted over who should have control over the cabin.

Actions   I basically told everyone, go back to your corners, let me figure out what the different needs and interests are, and we'll come back to review some proposed solutions. I mediated a dialogue between everyone because it had really disintegrated into self-interest.

Thinking   Someone had to be the adult, so I stepped into the role of peacemaker.

Outcome   We settled on one person who should hold the deed, and we drew up an agreement which made the cabin equivalent to a timeshare. The solution really resembled how it had functioned when my uncle was living.

Learnings   The vacuum created by one member's absence creates ambiguity that can bring out a less attractive side of human nature—selfish, petty behavior. In situations like that, it's important to defuse the tension, take the emotion out of it, and restore some reason. It's important to keep the big picture in mind—I didn't want to see the family have a falling-out over this.

Application When I come across situations where emotions run high, I understand better how to manage the emotion, reframe the problem, define what is the real issue. And I'm comfortable taking a command presence in charged and ambiguous situations.

What about this candidate's example seems to indicate a high level of People Agility?

When a candidate has high People Agility, you might notice that he or she...

Open Minded

Recognizes, appreciates, and is intrigued by differences

Is quick to learn from others' perspectives

Surrounds self with complementary skills and opinions

People Smart

Is insightful into the motives behind others' actions

Reads people and can articulate their qualities, perspectives, strengths, and weaknesses

Shows a sincere desire to understand where others are coming from and actively seeks out others' points of view

Situational Flexibility

Is adept at sizing up the situation and determining the most productive route to take

Probes interpersonal situations for meaning, and tries to fill in the blank spaces in his or her understanding

Actively seeks exposure to different people and situations to develop additional wisdom and insights into dealing with people-related matters

Agile Communicator

Is capable of using multiple influence tactics, and adjusts approach accordingly

Recognizes that influence is part logic and part relationships

Can clearly explain his or her thinking and tailor the message

Conflict Manager

Is adept at handling conflict, and would rather work through conflicts than avoid them

Keeps in mind the conflicting and overlapping needs of various constituents

Helps Others Succeed

Lets others shine

Finds ways for others to contribute

Watch out for overuse

Too much People Agility isn't necessarily a good thing. Overusing People Agility can lead to a desire to please everyone and let people considerations drive out other considerations in a situation. People who overuse People Agility can be perceived as waffling, overly accommodating, or unassertive.

When a candidate overuses People Agility, you may hear comments like...

"I'm not sure... I don't want to step on any toes or do something that might offend people."

"I always focus on talking through people's concerns, even if we have to set aside our meeting agenda."

"When I sense that something isn't working, the first thing I do is change my approach or my demeanor."

In the rare case of overuse, you might notice that he or she...

Needs to recognize more quickly when to implement a more firm, aggressive stance

May be perceived as being too eager and direct when approaching conflict

Can overemphasize cooperation and engage in more dialogue and bargaining than the situation merits

Needs to be careful that a deft approach to dealing with others isn't seen as manipulative

Typical People Agility

When a candidate has typical People Agility, you may hear comments like...

"I can build confidence
and satisfaction and
skill in others."

"I like to see
behaviors across time,
not just a snapshot."

"I put a filter on
what people tell me—
I have to be careful
not to get tainted."

Candidates who are typical in People Agility may share examples in interviews like this one about getting face time.

Situation   A year ago, I had to coach a CEO of a large organization who had a disengaged team. We needed to increase his awareness, improve his leadership style, and increase the team's effectiveness.

Actions   I needed face time with him, but formal meetings kept getting pushed off the calendar, so I joined him on an international flight. I made it a business imperative to become best friends with his admin, and once the admin understood the importance of our work, prioritized my calls and my time with the CEO. I also made it a point to meet with everyone on the team.

Thinking   It was important to meet face-to-face to build trust. And meeting with team members was essential. It added so much to my understanding of the situation.

Outcome   The CEO tried to manipulate my perception of the situation, but because I had multiple perspectives, I was able to keep him honest. The team dynamic improved.

Learnings   Even though I was hired to give feedback and coaching, I needed to seek out coaching and feedback for myself by checking in and troubleshooting with colleagues.

Application Since then, I have been careful to set clear expectations with the CEOs that I coach, and I check in with colleagues and mentors more regularly.

What about this candidate's example suggests a typical amount of People Agility?

When a candidate has typical People Agility, you might notice that he or she...

Open Minded

Observes and learns from other people

Purposefully focuses on being curious and asking good questions to both learn and influence others

People Smart

Has some favored approaches for dealing with others, but is able to size up an audience and is aware when the approach needs to be adjusted

Is fairly adept at considering others' needs, feelings, and perspectives

Seeks out key decision makers, engages them by building rapport, and has a sense for how to work with them

Forms decent insights, but could sometimes be sharper and more nuanced in perceptions of others' strengths and weaknesses

Situational Flexibility

Is attentive to the dynamics of power and influence; sensitive to the political landscape

Sets the tone in interactions, and tries to address conflicts and sensitive situations in a constructive manner

Agile Communicator

Strives to make sure logic and underlying principles are clearly understood by different audiences

Consults with others regularly to check thinking and hear different perspectives

Puts forth his or her point of view, and aims to maintain a productive back-and-forth dialogue in hopes of reaching some new solutions

Conflict Manager

Is diplomatic but genuine in approach to communicating and engaging people

Is somewhat selective in pursuing opportunities to engage in more direct conflict (i.e., chooses battles)

Helps Others Succeed

Believes in equipping and then empowering people, but could build deeper mentoring relationships to help them succeed

Recognizes and leverages others' individual strengths, but can overlook nuances

Low People Agility

When a candidate has low People Agility, you may hear comments like...

"I don't like telling people things they don't want to hear."

"People who don't know me as well—I come across as being too direct or not relationship-based. I underestimated the relationship culture here."

"When I got here and I was new, I remember thinking 'If I have to "partner" with one more person, I'm going to lose my mind.'"

When a candidate has low People Agility, you may hear examples in interviews like this one about ghostwriting.

Situation   I was in charge of writing a column for a senior leader. The approval process was grueling. After three or more rounds, I did not have approval yet—the reviewers didn't like the content, messaging, or tone. I let my frustration show, probably more than I should have.

Actions   I didn't know what to do, so I went to my boss. We decided that I had to sit down one-on-one with the senior leader to understand the feedback and then rewrite the column from scratch.

Thinking   It made sense for the person with the byline to have input earlier in the process.

Outcome   Direct access to the senior leader helped my understanding of the project—that the messaging was part of a larger change effort. We got a 40% click rate on the column.

Learnings   If you are going to write for someone, you need to understand that person's point of view.

Application   I haven't had the chance to apply this learning in other situations; this is the only person that I am writing for.

What do you notice about this example that indicates a low level of People Agility?

When a candidate has low People Agility, you might notice that he or she...

Open Minded

Doesn't dig deep to understand the ins and outs of others' points of view when he or she disagrees

People Smart

Perceives others' behaviors, but is not as clear on underlying motivations

Struggles to build trust and credibility with others

Manages personal brand very carefully; may benefit from letting guard down more often and showing some vulnerability

Situational Flexibility

Can get caught flat-footed and feel anxiety over high-complexity, high-stakes people situations

Overlooks social and political subtleties in favor of a rational, commonsense approach to working through situations with others

Needs to allow more space in interactions for others to take the lead and influence the tempo

Has a narrow definition of business problems and implications, and fails to include the people component

Agile Communicator

Demonstrates a fixed, default approach
and style in every situation

Has such a desire to get a point across and influence that he or
she can sometimes overwhelm or be seen as manipulative

Overuses rational argument as a means of persuading others, when
connecting on an emotional and inspirational level would be more effective

Conflict Manager

Shies away from situations that require decisions
that are difficult or contentious

Frames dialogue in terms of debate, disagreement, and right
versus wrong; views options in black-and-white terms

May personalize conflict to some degree

Helps Others Succeed

Could more quickly seek out others' needs, and explore
ways to add value to what they are doing

Misses opportunities to leverage others, collaborate, and
incorporate multiple perspectives into a single solution

Appears to be either overly self-reliant
or overly dependent on others

To become better at assessing People Agility, it helps to work on your own People Agility. As you reflect on situations that candidates shared with you in the course of the Learning Agility interview, consider how you would have responded in a similar situation and why. Take the opportunity of evaluating others' People Agility to evaluate and improve your own. For more ideas, check out *Becoming an Agile Leader*.

Once you've assessed the level of People Agility the candidate has, put that in context of the role he or she is interviewing for. What part does People Agility play in that role? Is it a position that requires working with new and different people, pinpointing other people's strengths and weaknesses, adjusting leadership and communication style to fit the audience? If so, People Agility will be mission critical.

"Don't address their brains.

Address their hearts."

– Nelson Mandela

Learning Agility Factor

The extent to which
an individual likes change,
continuously explores new
options and solutions, and
is interested in leading
organizational change efforts

Change
Agility

Promoting New Possibilities

Change Agility:
Promoting New Possibilities

Change agile people have the tendency to ask "what if?" and tinker with new ideas for the purpose of seeing continuous improvement. They move creative solutions from concept to adopted practice. And they are able to handle the heat and scrutiny that come with being cutting edge and leading change efforts.

Examples

Reveling in new ideas and possibilities

Challenging the status quo

Embracing risks

Testing and refining creative ideas

Seeking continuous improvement

Staying calm under pressure and uncertainty

Bringing others along by managing their
resistance to change

Recognizing Change Agility in Others

Change Agility is one of the hardest of all factors to discern in the context of a Learning Agility interview. Change Agility involves a couple of distinct skills: seeing the possibility of change and taking the idea from vision to reality. Someone who is high in Change Agility is able to see the current state and envision the possibilities beyond the status quo. They are open to unconventional ideas, willing to challenge established ways of thinking, and generate a broad, future-oriented vision. Seeing the possibility of change is at the essence of being change agile. Imagination and vision are prerequisites to experimenting with possibilities and being change agile.

The other part of being change agile is putting the new idea into practice and understanding what it takes to transform something from vision to reality. Being on the forefront of change requires tremendous leadership. It requires the ability to communicate the vision—getting people to embrace the need for change and rally to work for change. But it also requires being empathetic to people's change experience and being sensitive to the fact that others might not share the same commitment to go into the breach. Change agile people recognize that other people don't think like they do, but they find ways to bring them along. Being a change leader requires a fortitude that can withstand the slings and arrows that tend to fly in the direction of a person who challenges the way things have always been done.

Change Agility means both having the vision and ushering the vision into reality. But in Learning Agility interviews, it's common to see candidates who are strong in one area but not in the other area. Some candidates might be grand visionaries, but only in their own heads. They might be really good at generating great options, but fall down when it comes to following through. Or, maybe they try to be self-reliant when it comes to change, and they take a "build it and they will come" attitude. A few loyal followers might soak up the unorthodox vision but, in general, the effort rests on an army of one. This doesn't work forever. Change leadership is not effective when the committed inner circle is too small. Another problem can arise if a person views himself or herself as superior and treats others with palpable condescension, making other people's buy-in to the vision fleeting, at best.

Other candidates may be excellent at capitalizing on someone else's vision and making it happen, but lack a personal sense of vision. It is a valuable skill to be able to execute on a vision, make the idea work, and make change happen through the machinery of an organization. In this case, however, the problem is that people may see this person as a mouthpiece for someone else's vision, at which point there may be less commitment to the change effort. The ability to execute on a vision is a skill that is more plentifully available in the general population. When you're assessing Change Agility, the essence you are looking for is more the ability to envision an alternative future.

"My greatest challenge has been to change the mindset of people. Mindsets play strange tricks on us. We see things the way our minds have instructed our eyes to see."

Muhammad Yunus – Bengali founder of Grameen Bank

A Portrait of Change Agility:
Interviewing Muhammad Yunus

Muhammad Yunus is someone who is very high in Change Agility. When it came to fighting extreme poverty, Yunus saw both the need and possibility of change and was able to implement a transformative solution in the microlending movement he established. In the following interview with Andrew Denton, listen for how Yunus frames his vision of alternatives.

Denton When you took your idea of lending money to the poorest people to the banks because you thought they could help. What was their response?

Yunus So I went to the bank and I propose to the bank that the manager should lend money to the poor people. He fell from the sky, he couldn't believe it. He said, "Are you in your right mind that you are asking me to do that? Banks can not lend money to the poor people." Why not? Because they are not credit worthy. After about eight months I came up with another idea—I want to be guarantor, I'll sign all your papers, the risk is on me. So this time it's their language and not my language.

Denton You broke with the long established theory that the poorest people, you can't lend to them because they never repay you. It turned out not to be true.

Yunus Absolutely. I mean after all these 33 years of work, now is a good time to ask that question. Today Grameen and microcredit works all over the world lending money to the poor people. And it works perfectly. We lend money to the people, jobless people, women—100% of them are women.

They pay us back—repayment rate is 99.3%, without collateral, without guarantee, without any lawyers, beautifully.

Poverty is not created by the poor people. It is not their fault that they are poor. Poverty is created by the system, imposed on good blooded human beings and we can peel it off. Today I can almost say that almost two-thirds of the world population are rejected by the conventional banking system for no fault of their own. I said, banks come and tell us that you are not credit worthy, I said, shouldn't it be the other way round? The people should be telling whether the banks are people worthy.

Denton   Almost all of your clients are women and you describe how for a woman to get a loan, of say $15, they are trembling, they are shaking. How much courage did it take for a woman to accept these loans?

Yunus   It took six years to build that courage because she said, "I don't want to do that. I am afraid to touch money." So we literally carried some money with us to let her touch, "Why don't you touch it? Here is money, it's just a piece of paper, what's so scary about it?"

Used with permission. From "Muhammad Yunus." *Elders with Andrew Denton* [Television Series]. Andrew Denton. (2009, December 7). Sydney: Australian Broadcasting Corporation. Retrieved from http://www.abc.net.au/tv/elders/transcripts/s2757468.htm

Muhammad Yunus brought change to the way the world thinks about credit. Previously, access to credit was based on cultural, political, and financial norms. Yunus questioned the assumptions underlying the most basic banking function—lending money. Not only did he see an alternative future, he tirelessly advocated for the change required to make it a reality. Today, there are numerous microlending institutions that recognize the value of providing small loans to individuals without collateral, resulting in some of the lowest default rates in the industry. Yunus is an exceptional example of Change Agility to uphold, and he gives us all something to be inspired by and to strive for. Most people you interview will possess a more moderate level of Change Agility. Take a look at the examples of high, typical, and low Change Agility to find out what to look for, what to listen for, and how to assess candidates on this factor.

"I said, banks come and tell us
that you are not credit worthy,
I said, shouldn't it be the other way round?
The people should be telling
whether the banks are people worthy."

– Muhammad Yunus

High Change Agility

When a candidate has high Change Agility, you may hear comments like...

"I spend all day, all night, and every morning thinking of better ways to do things."

"I'm good where innovation is needed or nontraditional ways to get around (a problem)."

"I lean toward things that aren't status quo. I enjoy people and things that aren't typical."

Candidates who are high in Change Agility may share examples in interviews like this one about herding cattle.

Situation   My team was good, but complacent. You know, stick to the rules, not a lot of risk taking or originality. When our annual team-building time came around, I decided to shake things up.

Actions   I cajoled a local rancher to let me bring my team to his ranch for a day of cattle herding. People thought I was insane. They were in disbelief. I really had to convince them that this would be an incredible experience.

Thinking   I just thought, "What is the craziest thing I can do?" I'm an outdoor person, I like an adrenaline rush, the team needed to think differently, and I thought this would be just the thing to shock the system.

Outcome   It turned out to be a great experience. The team was really resistant initially, but in the end, it was a challenging, engaging, energizing experience that really lifted their spirits—in a way no one predicted.

Learnings   I was able to make an impact, but I realized that I need to be careful not to take people too far out of their comfort zone all at once. It really reinforced the importance of finding a gentle, facilitative approach to get people to come along with an idea.

Application I have had opportunities to shake things up since then, and while I don't suppress my instinct to bring about change, I meet people where they are and move them swiftly without jarring them. I focus on building the inspiration and purpose of the change. And I check my rearview mirror regularly to make sure I'm not leaving anyone behind. I know how to bring people along. I just need to remember to do it.

What about this candidate's example seems to indicate a high level of Change Agility?

When a candidate has high Change Agility, you might notice that he or she...

Continuous Improver

Is impatient for change—often not content with the status quo and willing to challenge established ways of doing things

Visioning

Thinks in possibility; is not constrained by past approaches or long-standing traditions

Trusts own convictions, but also welcomes differences of opinion and challenges to ideas

Is nimble; adjusts vision and approach as new information comes to light

Experimenter

Gets a thrill out of doing something that hasn't been done before

Presents unconventional, fresh alternatives, and models different scenarios

Prefers the autonomy to experiment, question conventional wisdom, and try things his or her own way

Welcomes new experiences; adapts calmly and effectively to changing situations

Innovation Manager

Builds strong esprit de corps, and is effective at getting others
to align around a common purpose in like-minded followers

Brings people along as new ideas are forming; plants seeds
and seeks input long before a change impacts people

Devotes time and attention to being transparent
and creating involvement and alignment

Frames change messages in an energetic
and compelling manner

Effectively navigates organizations to
put ideas into practice

Comfort Leading Change

Is empathetic to people's reactions to change, but also
willing to challenge others and put them to the test

Is not afraid of crisis, controversy, or resistance; is resilient
and tenacious in the face of difficulties

Is motivated to tackle big challenges; is cognizant of the challenges
faced with managing change and willing to bear the burden

Has the courage to take on change initiatives of
significant scale and scope

Is not afraid to stand alone and be in the vanguard

Watch out for overuse

Too much Change Agility isn't necessarily a good thing. Overusing Change Agility can lead to taking risks and making changes without weighing the overall benefits and drawbacks. People who overuse Change Agility can be perceived as lacking focus, being reckless, or disregarding potential consequences.

When a candidate overuses Change Agility, you may hear comments like...

"I generate a ton of ideas and, even if they aren't fully baked, I like to try them out."

"I don't have the patience to coax people to accept every little change."

"I like to push the boundaries on change— if you're not going to be bold, why bother?"

In the rare case of overuse, you might notice that he or she...

Itches for change opportunities
and may initiate change
for change's sake

Is too enthralled with
own vision; does not
stay grounded

May need to increase sensitivity
to others' need to process and adapt
to change at a different pace

May sometimes need to dial back
on the scope and intensity of change
efforts to keep people feeling
comfortable and bought-in

Typical Change Agility

When a candidate has typical Change Agility, you may hear comments like...

"I hate it when someone who is making a change does not realize the impact to the larger organization and the morale that goes with it."

"If I have some sort of safety net, I am willing to forge ahead when there is no road map, no operating manual."

"I would say I'm more energized by change than I am resistant to it, unless it comes all at once."

Candidates with typical Change Agility may share examples in interviews like this one about a pig named Bacon.

Situation   My roommate and I decided to buy a pig as a pet.

Actions   We bought a pig and we named it Bacon.

Thinking   We thought it would be fun and different to have a pet pig. We wanted to have something novel and interesting to show our friends when they came over to hang out.

Outcome   This did not turn out in any way how we thought it would. The pig ate a lot. And grew a lot. The pig started to smell, and our friends stopped coming over. The cute little pig got less cute. The apartment got to be quite a mess. It got expensive, and it wasn't that much fun. We ended up selling the pig to a farmer.

Learnings   We just didn't realize what we had gotten ourselves into. It's a serious responsibility taking care of livestock in your home. I learned that new adventures require some planning—you need to be aware of and examine the risks and possible negative outcomes. Ideas need to be examined before they are put into action.

Application   At work, I have a lot of interesting ideas and things I want to pursue, but I know I can't just dive in. I need to give it a little thought, build a business case, make sure that the change will be worth the trouble it might cause. I've definitely learned to channel my willingness to experiment. I would say that now I'm open to risks, but I'm not as naïve when I take risks.

What about this candidate's example suggests a typical amount of Change Agility?

When a candidate has typical Change Agility, you might notice that he or she...

Continuous Improver

Is willing to challenge others' perceptions and beliefs

Can explore alternatives and find win-win outcomes

Visioning

Is more incremental and pragmatic than bold and inventive in establishing a vision

Is good at spotting and capitalizing on trends, but may not be at the forefront of anticipating or creating paradigm shifts

Has some ability to project scenarios into the future

Is willing to push hard for personal beliefs and convictions

Experimenter

Is willing to experiment with new ideas, but with somewhat known implications

Will stretch risk taking and will experiment under pressure, but watches very closely for outcomes

Is willing to be proven wrong about a change effort or approach

Innovation Manager

Keeps an eye on both the big picture and the small picture

Tries to emphasize the benefits of change to others

Is sensitive to the difficult nature of change, and seeks
to guide others and involve them in the process

Tends to let things evolve, rather than actively manage change

Can take an idea and get it implemented

Is attentive to getting key stakeholders involved
and works to gain support for key initiatives

Is not a natural innovator, but can effectively
champion someone else's vision

Comfort Leading Change

Demonstrates some resiliency and pushes ahead
in the face of challenges and setbacks

May get deterred by others' reactions to change; needs to
develop thicker skin for dealing with others' criticisms and
concerns while still being responsive

Is becoming more comfortable dealing with change and
ambiguity that affects him or her directly

Is willing to take personal responsibility (to some extent)
for the consequences of change

Low Change Agility

When a candidate has low Change Agility, you may hear comments like...

"If someone comes
in with a different idea,
I might be a little hesitant."

"I love my work,
I love my team,
I love my manager.
I think, 'Why rock
the boat?'"

"For me, not having the
resources and working so
hard to get a lot of buy-in
for ideas sometimes kills
innovation because I have
to work so hard to get
a blessing."

Candidates who are low in Change Agility may share examples in interviews like this one about a group project.

Situation   In graduate school, I worked on a final group project—a case study. The group decided on an approach, but three people in the group went off, disregarded the agreed-upon approach, and changed the approach.

Actions   I was upset. I had already done some prep work. Most people thought the new way was better. We had a heated debate, and I was overruled.

Thinking   I didn't want to be the agitator in the group, and I value consensus decision making, so I went along with the decision to change the approach.

Outcome   We had more conflict and had trouble agreeing on what to present, who should present. The only thing we were aligned on was our motivation to deliver a quality product—which we did.

Learnings   It's best to clarify roles and responsibilities. We need to address conflict to get back on the same page. And placing people in their sweet spots is better than arbitrarily handing out tasks.

Application I recommend these ideas to others, but I have found it difficult to take these lessons and apply them where I work. There are a lot of politics involved, and my work teams are usually too big. It's really only something you can apply when you have a common goal.

What do you notice about this example that indicates a low level of Change Agility?

When a candidate has low Change Agility, you might notice that he or she...

Continuous Improver

Doesn't immediately pick up on a broken system or a need to change

Is comfortable doing things the way they've been done with some incremental improvement

Tends to be more reactive than proactive in approach to change; only engages once change is imminent

Visioning

Draws more off of what is known versus presenting an original slant; future vision is anchored to the here and now

Can see the direction where things are headed, but still needs to work on transforming insights into a compelling vision

Experimenter

Has limited ability to generate multiple scenarios and ways of doing things, or in bringing fresh thinking to all discussions

Is unwilling to look at solutions beyond comfort zone; prefers the tried-and-tested formulas

Prefers safer, simpler approaches where the outcome is more or less predictable

Innovation Manager

Needs practice balancing big-picture thinking with the finer aspects of planning, especially as the scope of change efforts increase

Has difficulty bringing everyone along, not just those that fall more readily into his or her camp

Could be more proactive in surfacing others' perspectives and concerns, and actively making them a part of the change process

Is still learning to refine the change message and adapt it for different audiences

Comfort Leading Change

Is willing to try out something new and different, so long as it has the support of other people

Is tentative and maps out approach to change very carefully, often favoring planning and building support over swift and decisive action

Is not resilient enough to handle the pressures involved in a "change agent" role, especially if it puts him or her in a lone position

To become better at assessing Change Agility, it helps to work on your own Change Agility. As you reflect on situations that candidates shared with you in the course of the Learning Agility interview, consider how you would have responded in a similar situation and why. Take the opportunity of evaluating others' Change Agility to evaluate and improve your own. For more ideas, check out *Becoming an Agile Leader*.

Once you've assessed the level of Change Agility the candidate has, put that in context of the role he or she is interviewing for. What part does Change Agility play in that role? Is it a position that requires creating and implementing a vision, changing strategic direction, or starting something new? If so, Change Agility will be mission critical.

"Why not?"

– Muhammad Yunus

Learning Agility Factor

The degree to which
an individual is motivated by
challenge and can deliver results
in first-time and/or tough
situations through resourcefulness
and by inspiring others

Results

Agility

Making Things Happen

Results Agility:
Making Things Happen

Results agile people are motivated by challenge and can deliver results in new and tough situations. Their intense drive and strong presence often inspire others to high achievement. With nimbleness, dexterity, and deftness, results agile people achieve results despite obstacles.

Examples

Getting things done under difficult, new, or ambiguous conditions

Motivating and inspiring others

Meeting obstacles with perseverance and resilience

Being adaptable and resourceful

Instilling confidence in others

Recognizing Results Agility in Others

Results agile people are like water when it comes to navigating obstacles. Water will go over, under, around, and through. Water carves through rock and breaks down dams. People high in Results Agility have their sights set on a goal, and they are going to reach it some way, somehow, as if by the sheer force of their will they can make it happen. Their doggedness and resourcefulness enable them to deliver against the odds.

Results Agility is the most commonly observed factor of all the Learning Agility factors. And it's one of the easiest factors to tip into overuse. If you sense that a candidate operates at a furious and frantic pace and achieves the goal but leaves collateral damage in his or her wake, you are seeing a clear sign of overuse.

The key to finding people who are most results agile is distinguishing those who use straight perseverance versus those who are clever and adaptable. High results agile people view failure as both a challenge and an opportunity to learn. After getting knocked down, they come back for more—but with a different approach. Watch for how the person learns from what doesn't work, learns it quickly, and doesn't make the same mistake twice.

Another indicator of high Results Agility is inspiring others to achieve great things. Getting results on your own is one thing; leading the charge with a whole band of people, motivating them to do what they might think is impossible or even crazy, and then getting the result against all odds is a hallmark of high Results Agility.

"You cannot keep determined people from success.
If you place stumbling blocks in their way,
they will use them for stepping-stones
and climb to new heights."

Mary Kay Ash – American entrepreneur

A Portrait of Results Agility:
Interviewing Mary Kay Ash

Mary Kay Ash is one person who embodied Results Agility. Her childhood, personal life, and financial situation, not to mention the cultural context of the time (1950s), conspired to make it very difficult for her to be a successful businesswoman. But she overcame obstacles and in the process changed the lives of thousands of women who didn't think they could achieve financial stability and independence by having a career. Notice how her Results Agility comes through in this *60 Minutes* segment from 1979 with Morley Safer.

Ash   My objective was just to help women; it was not to make a tremendous amount of sales. I want women to earn money commensurate with men. I want them to be paid on the basis of what they have between their ears—their brains....

Two of our girls this year, and I think this is phenomenal, reached the million-dollar mark in earnings. And this is less than 15 years (in business). This is not on sales, I'd like to make that clear, this is when you progress up that ladder to the point where you are helping teach other women to go out and do a tremendous job.

Safer   What do you think those women would have done otherwise, without this, without you?

Ash   They would be home looking at *Days of Our Lives* [a daytime television show].

Used with permission. From "1979: Making Millions the Mary Kay Way." *60 Minutes Overtime* [Television Series]. Morley Safer. (2011, April 15).
Retrieved from http://www.cbsnews.com/8301-504803_162-20054287-10391709.html

Mary Kay Ash is an exceptional case. It's not your average person who takes her personal savings of $5,000, starts a business, sees it grow to millions in a few short years, and empowers thousands of employees. Ash had the presence to inspire countless others to be their best and achieve results beyond what they thought possible. Take a look at the following behaviors, examples, and assessments that can help you detect high, typical, and low Results Agility in the candidates you interview.

"Never rest on your laurels.
Nothing wilts faster than
a laurel sat upon."

– Mary Kay Ash

High Results Agility

When a candidate has high Results Agility, you may hear comments like...

"The foundation of my career is building people and motivating them to do more than what they think they are capable of doing."

"I've received feedback that I'm the go-to guy to get around roadblocks. I find opportunities where others can't; I navigate the obstacles."

"I told them I would do it, but that they needed to leave me alone and let me and my team do it. We did $100 million last year, and we'll do more this year."

Candidates who are high in Results Agility may share examples in interviews like this one about banding together.

Situation   I got a special assignment in the facilities division to design all aspects of a new structure that was being assembled on the company's property. It was a small structure, but the specs were challenging and the time line was aggressive. I'm a trained accountant, I've done stints in HR and IT, and now I was going to manage construction.

Actions   I gathered all of the different tradespeople—plumbers, electricians, backhoe operators, carpenters. I worked with them to put together a construction plan, but all of the foremen were saying, "This can't be done." They were really giving me attitude, but I needed them to rally. I explained the purpose behind it, and I told them, "We don't have an option not to do this. You think the time lines and resources are crazy, but we have to give this our best shot. We owe it to ourselves to give it our best effort." I even rolled up my sleeves and did any job I was allowed to do—everything from getting donuts and coffee, to developing the project plan, to designing the electrical system, to troubleshooting when we found asbestos on-site.

Thinking   I figured if I showed that I was willing to do what it takes, that would be motivating for the group. I wanted everyone to take pride in the project. We were all in this together, and by operating as a team, we were going to prove to everyone else that we could do it.

Outcome   Any challenge that was thrown at us just galvanized us. We banded together and we got it built.

Learnings   Being willing to play many different roles and do what needed to be done helped me build engagement and motivation in others. Managing a project like this is more than just project management—it's managing at the emotional, tactical, and strategic levels.

Application   I've taken unmotivated teams in tough circumstances, and once I am able to get people to take pride in a monumental effort, we become unstoppable.

What about this candidate's example seems to indicate a high level of Results Agility?

When a candidate has high Results Agility, you might notice that he or she...

Drive

Has a strong sense of passion and urgency

Is quick to take action, but usually thinks things through sufficiently

Has a sense of when to push and when to let things take their course

Is always striving, and continually raises the bar for self and others

Is eager for challenge, but also realistic about situational constraints and own limitations

Resourcefulness

Is resourceful; will find workarounds and draw off of others' capabilities to attack challenging situations

Is comfortable operating with limited resources and information

Remains goal-focused, but is flexible and adaptable in the methods to get there

Presence

Is a vigorous person with strong energy and stamina

Is confident, ambitious, and determined when tackling problems, without being arrogant

Has a strong presence and built a good reputation; uses credibility as a pull to get the right talent to team up

Inspires Others

Seeks out significant challenges, and can motivate self
and others to pursue them

Pushes hard for results, but is mindful of not going overboard
or negatively impacting others

Addresses both *what* and *why* when giving direction to others

Sets a clear direction and gives others freedom to implement

Delivers Against the Odds

Balances patience and persistence; isn't frustrated when initial
solutions don't work

Is resilient, tenacious, and composed in the face of difficulties;
can bounce back quickly from minor setbacks

Will constantly reassess both the problem and the objective,
and consider multiple options to overcome challenges

Watch out for overuse

Too much Results Agility isn't necessarily a good thing. Overusing Results Agility can lead to being overly ambitious, stretching resources too thin, and focusing on getting results at all costs. People who overuse Results Agility can be perceived as lacking empathy, losing perspective, and risking their own and others' well-being in order to satisfy their ambitions.

When a candidate overuses Results Agility, you may hear comments like...

"Some people find the frenetic pace challenging, but I love it and figure that they'll get used to it."

"I haven't slept in days—I've been working non-stop."

"I refuse to accept failure. I will not fail."

In the rare case of overuse, you might notice that he or she...

Has difficulty with accepting (eventual) failure; commits strongly to a goal and/or course of action, and may stick with the ship too long on occasion

Could better balance spontaneity and improvisation with focus and prioritizing

Needs to develop own emotional intelligence to be able to play a truly inspirational role and bring out the best in everyone

Runs the risk of overcommitting on deliverables which are too ambitious for the situation or the players

Needs to temper the fast-paced, forward-moving approach with more patience and reflection

Typical Results Agility

When a candidate has typical Results Agility, you may hear comments like...

"I love working with people who come up with great ideas and helping them figure out how to make it happen. Let's take down barriers and make it work."

"I played flute in band —what's the point of this instrument when no one can hear it. I want to play the drums! Drive a lot of change, create new business, and contribute to the bottom line."

"I do know what I want and what I have to do to get there."

Candidates who have typical Results Agility may share examples in interviews like this one about making last-minute adjustments.

Situation   I had taken on responsibility for field communication. One of the first things I had to do was plan a three-day conference for 1,400 people. This was scope and scale that I had never done in my whole life.

Actions   My first reaction was "I can't wait to figure this out!" I asked colleagues who had some experience with this to walk me through what works, what's challenging. I dug up evaluations of previous conferences to see what worked in the past.

Thinking   Just because it was my first time didn't mean I couldn't stand on the shoulders of those who came before me.

Outcome   Right before the conference, we had a significant leadership change. We had to reassess everything, and there were some dramatic content adjustments. We had to pivot, quickly.

Learnings   Beyond planning and running the conference, I realized that I could add more strategic value by advising the new president on key messages, sharing where the organization is hurting, and how he could earn big points quickly.

Application   I continue to create events that connect the leader to the audience. I love creating those moments for people. They learn something, they hear something, they're inspired.

What about this candidate's example suggests a typical amount of Results Agility?

When a candidate has typical Results Agility, you might notice that he or she...

Drive

Takes pride in a job well done and holds self to high standards

Is dedicated to hard work and expects the same of others

Enjoys working hard, especially when the vision and purpose are clear

Knows the lay of the land and will take reasoned risks to accomplish goals

Does not hesitate to take on new challenges and new areas of responsibility

Resourcefulness

Will draw off of other resources when in a jam; can usually find a way to make things happen

Identifies areas where there is room for improvement, and takes a lead in analyzing root causes and finding possible solutions

Likes to get multiple options on the table

Presence

Is energetic and self-confident, but also willing to acknowledge when he or she is new to something

Inspires Others

Can drive others to achieve results, but is still learning
the finer points of motivation and buy-in

Could sometimes be more overt in efforts to rally
others and recognize achievements

Delivers Against the Odds

Is reluctant to cut losses and cancel a project when it's failing

Is willing to slog through a lot of complexity and bureaucracy to
get things accomplished

Trusts gut instinct in working through difficult situations,
but isn't always able to articulate specifics that help
guide the approach to achieving results

Can rise to the occasion in a crisis situation

Low Results Agility

When a candidate has low Results Agility, you may hear comments like...

"I tend to be good at coming up with a plan and sticking with it, no matter what."

"The first thing I look for is clear direction and space to execute that direction. I appreciate when I know what I'm supposed to do."

"I really do respond to people who are clear and straightforward. I have had bosses who don't ever tell you exactly what they want. Tell me what you want."

Candidates who are low in Results Agility may share examples in interviews like this one about a (not-so) textbook project.

Situation   I had to implement a new technology system in a small company.

Actions   I followed standard project protocol and methodically planned out the tasks and milestones for the project. There were some hiccups along the way, so I really hunkered down to analyze every next step.

Thinking   I wanted to make it a textbook project, but it really wasn't. Getting it to conform to the set methodology was very challenging.

Outcome   The project stalled at one point. One of the key contracts expired because of this delay, and we had to stop to draw up a new agreement with the vendor. Eventually, we were able to launch successfully.

Learnings   If I could have gotten the right information from the stakeholders within our established time frames, I think things would have gone more smoothly.

Application Since then, I have been careful to communicate well in advance. And I make decisions extra carefully in terms of what the best next steps are for a given project.

What do you notice about this example that indicates a low level of Results Agility?

When a candidate has low Results Agility, you might notice that he or she...

Drive

Executes consistently to meet threshold standards and expectations, but doesn't push to exceed them

Performs well when required to repeat high performance in similar situations

Exhibits some perfectionist tendencies that get in the way of getting results

Resourcefulness

Tends to go to the same set of resources in the same order

Has a narrow focus on executing via one path, rather than considering alternative paths

Is overly planful and pragmatic when the situation calls for a more fluid, unconventional approach

Is not attuned to the realities of the situation and what is called for

Presence

Has a muted passion and reduced sense of urgency

Intermittently shows flashes of strong presence, but needs to be more clear and consistent

Inspires Others

Is overly collaborative and consensus-driven at the expense of boldly giving others a call to action

Gets bogged down in minutiae

Delivers Against the Odds

Is untested in ability to get results under more-complex, larger-scope, higher-stakes situations

Is not adept at handling ambiguous situations or unknowns; is paralyzed by not knowing

Seeks yet more information to make decisions while the problem or task gets bigger and bigger

Gets discouraged easily when a project experiences setbacks

To become better at assessing Results Agility, it helps to work on your own Results Agility. As you reflect on situations that candidates shared with you in the course of the Learning Agility interview, consider how you would have responded in a similar situation and why. Take the opportunity of evaluating others' Results Agility to evaluate and improve your own. For more ideas, check out *Becoming an Agile Leader*.

Once you've assessed the level of Results Agility the candidate has, put that in context of the role he or she is interviewing for. What part does Results Agility play in that role? Is it a position that requires overcoming tremendous obstacles, leading in a crisis, or achieving lofty goals? If so, Results Agility will be mission critical.

*"I want women to earn money
commensurate with men.
I want them to be paid on the basis
of what they have between their ears
—their brains…"*

– Mary Kay Ash

Selecting for Learning Agility:
How to Use the Learning From Experience™
Interview Guide

Everyone wants to know the secret of success,
and there is one.
It's called continuously learning to do
what you don't know how to do.

Mike Lombardo and Bob Eichinger – Founding partners, Lominger International

The essence of Learning Agility is the ability to seek out and learn from new, different, and challenging experiences. One of the best ways to find out what a candidate has learned from his or her experiences is to ask. David Campbell, a renowned psychologist who has developed numerous assessments and inventories, including the well-known Campbell™ Interest and Skill Survey, states that you cannot underestimate the importance of asking the right questions. As a researcher and coauthor of the Lessons of Experience study, Mike Lombardo was focused on asking executives the right questions. One outcome of that landmark research was a better understanding of how Learning Agility differentiates successful executives.[19]

The Learning From Experience™ Interview Guide methodology is part of the legacy from that early research. The series of questions aim to uncover key experiences, the lessons learned from those experiences, and the ability to apply those lessons in future situations. Evaluating the answers to the question "What did you take away from that experience?" is where the hard part begins. The most learning agile individuals will offer up lessons that show a noteworthy depth of reflection. Their lessons tend to be nuanced, complex, and insightful. As the interviewer, it is a good sign if you find yourself gaining wisdom from the experiences and lessons a candidate is sharing—probably an indicator that the candidate has a high degree of Learning Agility.

The Learning From Experience™ Interview Guide questions and prompts are designed to help you better assess candidates and their degree of Learning Agility. The interview methodology and structure is purposeful, and the intent is to make it easier to listen for and make note of Learning Agility through the examples, experiences, reflections, and lessons that a candidate shares in the course of the interview.

Conducting Interviews Using the Learning From Experience™ Interview Guide

There are three critical steps in the Learning Agility interview process.

The first step is preparation. Start by getting familiar with the role, the organization, and the Learning Agility related requirements for the job. It might be helpful to understand what helped or hindered the predecessor in that role. This provides useful context when you consider which factors to interview for, or how to prioritize the order of the factors in the interview.

The second step is conducting the interview. During the interview, clear your mind so that you can focus your eyes and tune your ears to the behaviors and qualities that are the marks of a learning agile individual. Here, it is important to shut out all distractions and focus on listening and recording what you hear. It is perfectly acceptable to build some rapport at the beginning of the interview; just because it is a structured interview doesn't mean that you need to be rigid or cold. Be sure to frame how the interview will be conducted, and ask if the candidate has any questions before you begin. Here are a few points you may choose to make to set appropriate expectations for the interview:

This is a specific approach to interviewing
and may not seem familiar.

I am going to ask you to recall past experiences.
It's most helpful if you can share a specific,
real-life example in response to each question.

Your response can draw upon work or non-work situations,
including school, community, or personal experiences.

Please take the time you need to think of your response.

I will be making some notes during our conversation.

In our experience, a typical interview to assess Learning Agility lasts about one hour. Each question and its corresponding follow-up questions take about 10 to 12 minutes, so you can expect to cover four or five Learning Agility factors. If you only have a very short time to get a read on someone's Learning Agility, in lieu of addressing the five factors, you can ask a question related to Overall Learning Agility or focus on the factors that are most mission critical for the role. Some interviewers prefer to spend up to two hours interviewing, or possibly even have multiple interviewers assess a candidate's Learning Agility and circle back for a calibration session. While these practices may enhance the accuracy and confidence of the ratings, they are not always practical and may be going above and beyond what is required to get a solid read on a candidate's Learning Agility for most situations.

The Learning Agility interview begins with a behavioral interview question—a question designed to prompt the candidate to recall a real and significant experience, one that invites deeper responses through follow-up questions. For example:

> Tell me about a time when you had to do something very challenging, and you didn't initially know how to do it.

Often, candidates assume that the experience needs to be work related. In most interview settings, that would make sense. In the case of interviewing for Learning Agility, however, both personal and professional examples are appropriate. It doesn't even necessarily need to be a recent experience. The candidate might recall a situation that occurred in college or graduate school or in his or her first job. Assure the candidate that these are valid options, and give the candidate time to think of the experience he or she would like to share with you. The richer and more potentially meaningful the experience, the more opportunity you have to get a glimpse into how the candidate's Learning Agility comes to life in specific situations.

The follow-up questions follow a logical sequence and get at the candidate's actions given the situation, the thinking behind his or her actions, what the outcome was, what was learned from the experience, and how that lesson has been applied since then. Each question should flow easily into your dialogue with the candidate and does not need to be delivered in an overly formal or verbatim manner to have the desired impact. Space is provided for notes, and the "Look and Listen" section of the interview guide provides themes to guide your attention during the interview.

Look and Listen for How the Individual:

Responds to new challenges

Solves problems

Gets things done through others

Implements change

Gets results

The third step of the interview process involves evaluating and rating the candidate. While you may form an initial, rough judgment during the interview, there are a few reasons for waiting until after the interview before completing the ratings. First, it is difficult to listen fully, neutrally, and objectively if you are also focused on making a judgment. Second, when the interview involves asking questions related to multiple factors of Learning Agility, it is quite common to hear aspects of Self-Awareness emerge from the answer to the People Agility question. Or, aspects of Change Agility surface during your reflection on the Results Agility section. Because the Learning Agility factors are independent but related—and because situations often require more than one type of agility—it can be advantageous to wait until after the interview to assess the candidate.

In some cases, it may be enough to say that the candidate possesses lower, typical, or higher Learning Agility. In other cases, a greater degree of precision may be optimal. In all cases, the more Learning Agility interviews you conduct, the more confident and precise you can be as you place each candidate along the spectrum of Learning Agility. Having more interview experiences of your own will provide you with reference points that help you view candidates relative to other people.

Take the appropriate time to review and compile your notes and findings, preferably in a quiet setting shortly after the interview. The "What I'm seeing and hearing" section for each of the Learning Agility factors is designed to help you do just that. Signs of low, typical, and high Learning Agility are summarized for each factor along with space to make your own notes about what you observed. A 5-point scale is provided in quarter-point increments for those who are inclined to be very precise, and a range is provided for where low, typical, and high Learning Agility scores should fall. Low scores range from 1.0 to 2.25, typical scores range from 2.5 to 3.5, and high scores range from 3.75 to 5.0. The page also includes a visual reminder that Learning Agility is distributed along a normal bell curve in the general population—just like height and weight. Some candidates may be very high or very low, but most candidates will fall somewhere in the middle, hence our use of the word "typical." When you've completed your ratings, use the "Observations and Scores" pages to record all of your observations and ratings in one place.

Not All Experiences and Lessons Are Created Equal

As explored in *Becoming an Agile Leader: A Guide to Learning From Your Experiences*,[20] some experiences are more developmental than others and provide more opportunity for developing mission-critical skills and Learning Agility. When you interview candidates, listen for whether the person's experiences are varied, intense, include working with diverse people, and involve some level of adversity. If you continue to hear the same type of mundane or typical experience over and over again as you move through the questions, that may be an indication of lower Learning Agility.

Challenging experiences tend to spark more learning and may include some of the following characteristics:

Success was not guaranteed

Responsibility rested with the person

Required working with new people or a lot of people

Stakes and pressure were high

Required influencing without authority

Different from what the person had done before

The person's work was under scrutiny

New territory for the organization or community

Required the person to be resourceful

Tested the person's ability to deal with complexity and ambiguity

Involved some hurdles or hardship

Experiences are not created equal, nor are the lessons that are derived from those experiences. Two people could experience the same situation and come away with very different levels of reflection and insight. If you hear lessons that sound cliché, simplistic, or obvious, those signal less-developed Learning Agility. When the lessons are rich, provide new insight, and help the person achieve a higher level of understanding, that is a sign of better-developed Learning Agility. For example, notice the difference between the following lessons two different candidates took from the same experience:

"I learned that I needed to communicate better."

"I realized that I needed to communicate more frequently and with some repetition. And, while it may seem counterintuitive, I learned that the best way to understand whether I've gotten my message across is to listen."

The first might strike you as an obvious platitude. When you read the second example, you may say to yourself, "Interesting, I never thought of it like that, but it makes sense." The difference between these two examples is just one illustration of the qualitative difference between the lessons learned by lower and higher learning agile individuals. A tip for when you solicit a candidate's lessons: feel free to ask, "Anything else?" to prompt any additional thoughts or insights they may have drawn from the situation.

When to Use the
Learning From Experience™ Interview Guide

The Learning From Experience™ Interview Guide can be used to assess Learning Agility for multiple purposes. Identifying learning agile individuals can be useful in the context of selection (for both external and internal candidates), high potential identification, and development.

Selection. Selecting internal or external candidates is the most common application of the Learning From Experience™ Interview Guide. When used for selection purposes, it is critical that organizations make sure that Learning Agility is an important success factor for the targeted job or role. As discussed earlier, all jobs are not created equal. Research indicates that high Learning Agility is required for organizational roles that involve[21]:

> Job transitions, such as assuming unfamiliar or new responsibilities, duties, and assignments

> Innovation or creating change, such as developing new directions, solving inherited problems, or start-up activities

> A high level of responsibility, such as being under the pressure of deadlines and being responsible for key, high-stakes, visible decisions

> Influencing others without authority or rank, such as gaining cooperation from peers or higher-level management, and/or managing and responding to pressures from external stakeholders

> Dealing with obstacles or difficulties, such as adverse business conditions, lack of organizational support, or confronting difficult people

There are several types of interviews used by recruiters, search consultants, and hiring managers when searching for the right candidate for a position. The Learning Agility interview is just one type of interview that would be used in some combination with other types of interviews, including:

A general screening interview

A functional/technical skills evaluation

A culture fit assessment

A competency interview

A sales interview, or the close

We typically recommend positioning a Learning Agility interview toward the end of the selection process. In this way, you can ensure that your time is invested well because you are using Learning Agility to differentiate a pool of candidates who are all viable and well qualified.

High Potential Identification. Identifying high potentials for the purpose of succession planning or development is another way the Learning From Experience™ Interview Guide is used in organizations. Individuals who have the most potential for future growth are those who tend to be good at Learning Agility.[22] While technical skills and intelligence are important, when a job tackles new or unknown territory, technical skills and intelligence will only get a person so far. In fact, relying solely on those assets, a person will inevitably get stuck at some point and rigidly rely on what worked for him or her in the past rather than experiment with new solutions.

Learning Agility is the quality that helps individuals learn new skills and behaviors. It helps individuals break free from old habits that don't work anymore, and it spurs them to bring about change when change is sorely needed. Learning agile individuals have more strategies to draw from when faced with a challenge, and if they can't find a strategy that works for the new context, they try something new. These are important considerations when identifying individuals who may take on bigger, broader, and more strategic roles in the organization.

Without a clear understanding of the criteria for identifying high potentials, there is more room for error. One type of error is the false positive—those who are identified as having potential but, in fact, are more technically proficient or deep experts who do one thing extremely well. (If these individuals want to succeed in more broad or general roles, they will need to further develop their Learning Agility.) The other type of error is the false negative—those people who have potential but are overlooked. Learning how to spot diamonds in the rough can help minimize this second type of error.

Using Learning Agility as part of your organization's high potential identification process can give leaders a common framework in which to discuss and decide potential. By using the Learning Agility definitions and behaviors along with the Learning From Experience™ Interview Guide or other Learning Agility assessments, leaders can identify those individuals who exhibit the qualifying criteria for having potential, including:

Solid performance in the current assignment, better than most

New behavioral skills acquired

Increase in technical and business savvy

A willingness to take on first-time challenges

Openness to feedback

Key challenges/tasks/assignments that were different or first time for them

Using an assessment of Learning Agility like the Learning From Experience™ Interview Guide can improve the quality and accuracy of high potential identification.

Development. Whether it's leadership skills, technical skills, or Learning Agility, in order to develop it, the person needs to get a sense of where they are today. Conducting a Learning Agility interview is one way to assess a person's current level of Learning Agility. In fact, the process of participating in the interview can spark reflection and garnering of new insights and lessons from the experiences being discussed. The questions and prompts in the Learning From Experience™ Interview Guide adapt well to coaching conversations and become a tool for reflection and development.

There are many more resources and tools for developing Learning Agility in individuals: for example, *Becoming an Agile Leader* offers development suggestions for each factor, and *FYI™ for Learning Agility* provides development suggestions for specific skills within each factor of Learning Agility. Regardless of the resources your organization uses to help individuals develop Learning Agility, one truism remains: We learn best by doing. Encourage people to continue to seek new and different experiences that stretch their skills and push them out of their comfort zones.

Using the Learning From Experience™ Interview Guide to Complement Other Learning Agility Assessments

The Learning From Experience™ Interview Guide is just one of the ways you can measure Learning Agility. In fact, there are three different assessments for measuring Learning Agility that we recommend. Depending on the purpose of the assessment and various organizational situations, companies can choose to administer the Learning From Experience™ Interview Guide, the Choices™ multi-rater assessment, or the viaEDGE™ self-assessment. No one assessment is the best. They are designed to accommodate different needs and priorities.

Each of these assessments offer different views into the same mission-critical quality—Learning Agility. You may choose to use them to complement each other. The Learning From Experience™ Interview Guide provides a nice, qualitative deep dive to accompany the initial read of a viaEDGE™ or Choices™ assessment. Or, if one factor or score is particularly important, you may wish to corroborate the initial assessment with a follow-up interview to understand in more detail the person's capability in that area.

The Learning From Experience™ Interview Guide can serve many purposes as organizations manage talent, including:

External selection

High potential identification

Leadership development

Internal promotion

Job assignments/deployment (e.g., international assignment, head of start-up business unit)

Regardless of how you and your organization choose to employ these Learning Agility assessments, the Learning From Experience™ Interview Guide offers a few key advantages. The qualitative nature of the assessment allows more texture and more nuance to come through about a person's Learning Agility. And the Learning From Experience™ Interview Guide is the only one of the three assessments which provides a window into how a person reflects upon and learns from his or her experiences. It gives you the clearest and most descriptive portrait of the person's Learning Agility in action.

Once you've assessed the level of Learning Agility for a candidate, it can be a helpful next step to consider how his or her level of Learning Agility translates into strengths and weaknesses and how those might affect performance on the job. If the candidate is offered the position, these observed strengths and weaknesses can be a helpful starting point for an onboarding plan. *Becoming an Agile Leader* is a great resource for building a development plan that can help the candidate accelerate his or her contribution in the new role and organization.

As you begin to conduct Learning Agility interviews, consider the interview process as a learning experience in and of itself. Interviewing a variety of candidates gives you, the interviewer, the opportunity to broaden your horizons, hear about many diverse experiences, and reflect on other people's lessons learned. The ability to get an accurate read on other people's strengths and weaknesses and their level of Learning Agility is a valuable—and somewhat rare—skill. Continue to reflect and add to your own lessons learned as you become a wise and savvy assessor, discerning Learning Agility in others.

Acknowledgments

We wish to express our appreciation to the many people who worked to make this book possible.

Thanks to Bob Eichinger and Mike Lombardo for the rich legacy of research, experience, and wisdom upon which this book and the Learning From Experience™ methodology are built.

Thanks to Vicki Swisher, Guangrong Dai, and King Yii (Lulu) Tang for reviewing drafts and being great thought partners in the creation of this book.

Thanks to Kim Ruyle, Nicole Lambrou, and Beth Summers for their feedback and ideas.

Thanks to the core team, including Zoe Hruby, Molly Hedlund, La Tasha Reed, Lesley Kurke, Doug Lodermeier, Paul Montei, Yasmin Salcedo, and Bonnie Parks, for their hard work and dedication.

Notes

Introduction

1. Hunter, J. E., & Hunter, R. F. (1984). Validity and utility of alternative predictors of job performance. *Psychological Bulletin, 96*(1), 72–98. doi:10.1037/0033-2909.96.1.72

2. Goleman, D. (1998). *Working with emotional intelligence.* New York, NY: Bantam.

3. De Meuse, K. P. (2011, October 20). What's smarter than IQ? *Proof Point.* Los Angeles, CA: Korn/Ferry Institute.

4. Swisher, V. V., Hallenbeck, G. S., Jr., Orr, J. E., Eichinger, R. W., & Lombardo, M. M. (in press). *FYI™ for learning agility* (2nd ed.). Minneapolis, MN: Lominger International: A Korn/Ferry Company.

5. Eichinger, R. W., & Lombardo, M. M. (2009). *High learners as high performers* [White Paper]. Minneapolis, MN: Lominger International: A Korn/Ferry Company.

6. Swisher, V. V. (2012). *Becoming an agile leader: Know what to do…When you don't know what to do.* Minneapolis, MN: Lominger International: A Korn/Ferry Company.

7. Lombardo, M. M., & Eichinger, R. W. (2011). *The leadership machine: Architecture to develop leaders for any future* (10th Anniversary edition). Minneapolis, MN: Lominger International: A Korn/Ferry Company.

The Science Behind Selection: Why We Can't Completely Trust Our Gut (or Our Mind)

8. Davis, D. M., & Hayes, J. A. (2012, July / August). What are the benefits of mindfulness? *Monitor on Psychology 43*(7), 64–70.

9. Kahneman, D. (2011). *Thinking, fast and slow*. New York, NY: Farrar, Straus and Giroux.

10. Gladwell, M. (2000, May 29). The new-boy network: What do job interviews really tell us? *The New Yorker*, p. 68.

11. Gladwell, M. (2009). The new-boy network: What do job interviews really tell us? In M. Gladwell (Author), *What the dog saw: And other adventures*. New York, NY: Little, Brown and Company.

12. Tsai, W. C., Chen, C. C., & Chiu, S. F. (2005). Exploring boundaries of the effects of applicant impression management tactics in job interviews. *Journal of Management, 31*(1), 108–125. doi:10.1177 / 0149206304271384

13. Matlin, M. W. (2009). *Cognition* (7th ed.). New York, NY: John Wiley and Sons, Inc.

14. Thorndike, E. L. (1920). A constant error in psychological ratings. *Journal of Applied Psychology, 4*(1), 25–29.

15. Jones, E. E., & Davis, K. E. (1965). From acts to dispositions: The attribution process in person perception. In L. Berkowitz (Ed.), *Advances in experimental social psychology* (Vol. 2, pp. 219–266). New York, NY: Academic Press. doi:10.1016 / S0065-2601(08)60107-0

16. Kahneman, D. (2011). *Thinking, fast and slow*. New York, NY: Farrar, Straus and Giroux.

17. Posthuma, R. A., Morgeson, F. P., & Campion, M. A. (2002). Beyond employment interview validity: A comprehensive narrative review of recent research and trends over time. *Personnel Psychology, 55*(1), 1–81. doi:10.1111/j.1744-6570.2002.tb00103.x

18. Wexley, K. N., Yukl, G. A., Kovacs, S. Z., & Sanders, R. E. (1972). Importance of contrast effects in employment interviews. *Journal of Applied Psychology, 56*(1), 45–48. doi:10.1037/h0032132

Selecting for Learning Agility: How to Use the Learning From Experience™ Interview Guide

19. McCall, M. W., Jr., Lombardo, M. M., & Morrison, A. M. (1988). The lessons of experience: *How successful executives develop on the job*. New York, NY: Free Press.

20. Orr, J. E. (2012). *Becoming an agile leader: A guide to learning from your experiences*. Minneapolis, MN: Lominger International: A Korn/Ferry Company.

21. McCauley, C. D., Ruderman, M. N., Ohlott, P. J., & Morrow, J. E. (1994). Assessing the developmental components of managerial jobs. *Journal of Applied Psychology, 79*(4), 544–560. doi: 10.1037/0021-9010.79.4.544

22. Lombardo, M. M., & Eichinger, R. W. (2011). *The leadership machine: Architecture to develop leaders for any future* (10th Anniversary edition). Minneapolis, MN: Lominger International: A Korn/Ferry Company.

References

Overall Learning Agility: Know What to Do When You Don't Know What to Do

Rose, C. (2008, February 12). A conversation with Richard Branson [Interview]. *Charlie Rose*. [Syndicated Public Broadcasting Service (PBS) television series episode]. Retrieved from http://www.charlierose.com/view/interview/8935; minute: 5:04–6:30

Self-Awareness: Seeking Personal Insight

Angelou, M. (1969). *I know why the caged bird sings*. New York, NY: Random House.

Angelou, M. (1976). *Singin' and swingin' and gettin' merry like Christmas*. New York, NY: Random House.

Winfrey, O. (2000, December). Oprah talks to Maya Angelou [Interview]. *O, The Oprah Magazine*. Retrieved from http://www.oprah.com/omagazine/Oprah-Interviews-Maya-Angelou/3#ixzz20Qf2IQfi

Mental Agility: Making Fresh Connections

Albert, D. (2011, January 14). An interview with Albert Einstein on science careers [Simulated Interview]. *Science Careers Blog*. Retrieved from http://blogs.sciencemag.org/sciencecareers/2011/01/an-interview-wi.html

Einstein, A., & Calaprice, A. (Ed.). (2011). *The Ultimate Quotable Einstein*. Princeton, NJ: Princeton University Press.

People Agility: Bringing Out the Best in Others

Mandela, N. (2010). *Conversations with myself* (pp. 325–326). New York, NY: Farrar, Straus and Giroux.

Winfrey, O. (2001, April). Oprah talks to Nelson Mandela [Interview]. *O, The Oprah Magazine.* Retrieved from http://www.oprah.com/world/Oprah-Interviews-Nelson-Mandela/7#ixzz20QwtP6Ai

Change Agility: Promoting New Possibilities

Denton, A. (2009, December 7). Interview with Muhammad Yunus [Interview]. *Elders with Andrew Denton.* [Television series episode]. Sydney: Australian Broadcasting Corporation. Retrieved from http://www.abc.net.au/tv/elders/transcripts/s2757468.htm

Results Agility: Making Things Happen

Safer, M. (2011, April 15). 1979: Making millions the Mary Kay way [Interview]. *60 Minutes Overtime.* [Television series episode]. Retrieved from http://www.cbsnews.com/8301-504803_162-20054287-10391709.html

Resources for Individuals

Learning Agility can be developed. Here are some tools that can help you on your journey to explore and build your Learning Agility.

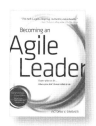

Becoming an Agile Leader: Know What to Do…When You Don't Know What to Do explores the five key characteristics, or factors, of Learning Agility. Spotlighting well-known leaders from business and the world stage, *Becoming an Agile Leader* is filled with more than 70 practical development tips you can start using today to increase your own agility and help ensure success in those new, challenging assignments. So you will know what to do…when you don't know what to do.

With *Becoming an Agile Leader: A Guide to Learning From Your Experiences*, you can explore the formative experiences that shaped the learning agile leaders profiled in the book *Becoming an Agile Leader*. This practical guide lets you reflect on your own experiences, past and present, and includes a comprehensive listing of on- and off-the-job experiences that will help you plan for assignments that build Learning Agility.

The *Becoming an Agile Leader* Reflections App can help you achieve greater self-awareness through capturing on-the-spot insights and reflections. The *Becoming an Agile Leader* Reflections App provides inspiring, thought-provoking quotes related to the Learning Agility factors which will help you easily reflect, document, and transfer lessons from your experiences.

FYI™ *for Insight* will help you understand 21 leadership characteristics for success and 5 characteristics that can derail your career. It will also make you aware of *why* you may be lacking skill or motivation in certain areas. This is critical because becoming self-aware can get you 50% of the way toward improving your performance.

Insight into strengths and weaknesses can help you get what you want from your career. The *FYI*™ *for Insight* Self-Awareness Assessment is a three-step process that takes just a few minutes. A personalized report gives you a self-awareness score and highlights your hidden strengths and blind spots.

More information on these resources can be found at http://www.lominger.com

Resources for Organizations

Research has clearly shown that Learning Agility is a primary component and key differentiator of potential for leadership roles. By understanding and leveraging Learning Agility in your organization, you can better distinguish between current performance and future potential and create a more targeted, differentiated development strategy for current and future leaders. The assessment and development tools here can help you integrate Learning Agility into your organization's strategic talent management initiatives.

Assessments

The Learning From Experience™ Interview Guide is a selection tool designed to assist employers with assessing learning agility in the interviewing process. The guide helps organizations build future bench strength through interviewing and selecting the most learning agile internal and external candidates.

The Choices™ multi-rater assessment has been used for years by organizations to identify, validate, and select those who are the most learning agile. Choices™ scores have been significantly related to independent measures or ratings of potential, consistent performance, and staying out of trouble. Other formats available and branded as part of the Learning Agility Architect™ suite are the Sort Cards and a Quick Score Questionnaire. *Available in multiple languages.*

viaEDGE™ easily and efficiently gauges the Learning Agility of large numbers of individuals, with the ease of an online self-administered assessment. viaEDGE™ helps organizations assess internal talent for placement and development of high potentials and can aid in external candidate hiring. *Available in multiple languages.*

Development Tools

Learning Agility can be developed. *FYI™ for Learning Agility* is designed for any motivated person seeking to develop skills that lead to increased Learning Agility. It includes 200+ improvement and workaround strategies that individuals can use today on or off the job.

More information on these resources can be found at http://www.lominger.com